# almost

## When Living for God Falls Short

By Dr. Berkley A. Baker

# Copyright

Copyright © 2019 Berkley A. Baker
All rights reserved.

eBook ISBN 978-1-7344832-2-2
Trade Paperback ISBN 978-1-7344832-0-8
Hardcover ISBN 978-1-7344832-1-5

Cover design by Jenée Baker; photography by CGinspiration / Getty Images

Published in the United States by CIMI Publishing, LLC

Library of Congress Control Number: 2020901450

"Every artist has thousands of bad drawings in them and the only way to get rid of them is to draw them out." – Chuck Jones

*Lord, You know my thoughts concerning You. You are aware of my shortcomings and shortsightedness. You are not caught off guard by my faults and my failures, yet You love me anyway. Over the past thirty years, you've edged me closer to this conversation, and now I sit on the brink of this work. Lord, if You are not part of this project, I ask for it to fail. If this work is not consistent with Your heart, I pray its message would fall upon deaf ears. But if it's true, I pray that You would be lifted up and glorified.*

*This book is dedicated to my wife and best friend, Jenée.
It's dedicated to my three wonderful children; you make
me better. And it's dedicated to the thirsty, those who have
hearts that pant after the Lord (Psalm 42:1), and to Abba
Father, who gives us a heart to know Him (Jeremiah 24:7).*

BERKLEY BB BAKER

# CONTENTS

Acknowledgments.................................................. 9

Preface.............................................................. 13

Introduction....................................................... 17

    Where is Jesus?............................................... 17

    Law-Abiding Citizen ....................................... 19

    Leaving Jesus Behind ...................................... 20

    A Model of Divine Nature ............................... 22

    This Book's Journey ....................................... 28

1. First Blend: Earthly Commander.................... 33

    A Desperate Father.......................................... 33

    Earthly Commander Nature Explained.......... 35

    Productivity and Belief.................................... 38

    Losing God in the Blessings ........................... 42

    The GMAT ..................................................... 45

    RECAP............................................................ 51

2. Second Blend: Heavenly Commander ............. 55

    A Frightful Jailer............................................. 55

    Heavenly Commander Nature Explained ...... 57

    Conforming to His Image ............................... 61

    Cognitive Christianity..................................... 67

    Ellie the Possum.............................................. 72

RECAP ................................................................. 74

3. A Shift: Growing Beyond Commands and Conformity 79

Garden Flavored............................................... 79

A Failed Shift.................................................. 83

Incongruence................................................... 86

Focus.............................................................. 89

Distant and Disconnected ................................. 91

From Commander to Companion ...................... 94

RECAP .......................................................... 96

4. Third Blend: Earthly Companion........................... 101

Damascus Road............................................... 101

Earthly Companion Nature Explained................ 104

Chrysalis and Coffin ....................................... 108

Transformation Interrupted.............................. 116

No Need to Walk Alone ................................... 118

RECAP .......................................................... 123

5. Fourth Blend: Heavenly Companion ..................... 127

Illicit Sex and Intimacy................................... 127

Heavenly Companion Nature Explained ............ 130

The Importance of Intimacy............................. 134

Purposely Intimate ......................................... 144

Purpose-filled Connection................................ 147

RECAP .......................................................... 150

6. Balanced & Complete........................................... 155

A Son, a Sibling, and a Father ..................................... 155

Two Departures ............................................................ 158

The Wholeness of God's Divine Nature ..................... 164

Conclusion ................................................................. 165

Endnotes...................................................................... 177

# ACKNOWLEDGMENTS

Lord, I'm grateful for the contributions of so many concerning this work. My friend and brother Col. Michael Davidson reminded me that this message has always been residing in me since West Point. My heart yearns for us, as His church, to make Him the center of our worship. I desire that Jesus would be the focal point of our gatherings. My cousin Missy and I would spend countless hours hashing out that very point. What would our communities look like if Jesus was our focus? How would we experience God corporately if our weekly services more closely reflected Mary sitting at the feet of Jesus? Missy, our conversations largely influenced this work. Thank you for enduring through my earlier drafts.

I am grateful for my wife, Jenée. You have endured every aspect of this work—needed rewrites, needless rewrites, writer's block, and tautologously writing. Babe, your mixture of tender words and constructive criticism was always needed and more appreciated today than ever before. Please accept my heartfelt thanks. Amarie, thank you for coming by to visit me in my office or welcoming an impromptu reading party just before you called it a night. I wrote this book for those who, like us, are learning how to thirst after God. To my daughter Amanda, you know I've been at this for a long time. Thanks for encouraging me and helping me to lock in the title. And Josiah, how the tables have turned. I recall

Mom laughing in the kitchen as you instructed me to "read that part again; it's a little unclear." Mom and Dad, I appreciate you guys reading through the rough versions. I'll never forget our two-hour conference call, hashing through some of the more challenging parts of this project.

God has blessed me with so many friends who allowed themselves to be interrupted to hear what God placed upon my heart. Kwala, thank you for listening impromptu at the kitchen table. Lee and Crystal, I appreciate you listening as your kids were preparing for bed. Bob, thank you for encouraging me to write as you were enduring chemo. Our brotherhood is eternal. Julia, you pointed me toward C.S. Lewis and helped me to think differently. Randy, you've been talking about this book for a while, at least since 2015. Thank you for persistent encouragement; although it was not always wanted, it was needed. I'd also like to thank Quinn, Andrew, Ellen, Eric, and Lolita for participating in the reading parties. They were productive and fun; without them, this endeavor would have stalled.

I am also grateful for the men of EncourageMen. At our 2019 Annual Retreat, we had an unexpected scheduling change. Leon Byrd, a co-founder of EncourageMen Ministry, shared that we needed someone to lead the Saturday evening discussion and asked if I would be willing. At the time, I felt as though the message of this book was overflowing the boundaries of my heart. It was like fire shut up in my bones. I was so grateful for the opportunity to share it with my brothers, not as a sermon but as a collective dialogue.

Our discussion sparked something in me, and it pushed me forward. Thank you! I'd like to thank my copy editor, Megan Ryan. She works at Upwork.com, and her contributions to this work were a godsend. I'm grateful for my beloved Aunt Carolyn, mother-in-law Joyce, Pastors Tony and Gwen Brock, Chris, Carmen, Kristine, my life group, the members of Hope and Life Fellowship, and so many others.

This list above is in no way exhaustive. Your words, thoughts, and prayers have contributed to the completion of this book. Much love and thanks for your support and efforts in helping me to do what I believe God called me to do.

# PREFACE

Initially, I was not going to include a preface for this book because I rarely read them myself. But I received some feedback from a friend that made me reconsider. This friend is somewhat of a savant: She is a talented editor and writer when she isn't speaking Quenya (a language invented by J.R.R. Tolkien). After reading a pre-published edition, she said, "You give no clue about who you are until thirteen pages into the book." She was right. Most of my life, I've sought obscurity. Apparently, this doesn't bode well for first-time writers. So, allow me to introduce myself.

Like many authors, events from my childhood influenced my writing. Most of my early years, I lived with my maternal grandparents. They were very active in their local church. If the doors to the sanctuary were open, we were there. Even when I was little, I was a curious thinker. I was five years old when I first heard the hymn entitled "I Need Thee Every Hour."[i] Its opening lyrics perplexed me, and I remember thinking, "What is the O, and why do we need it?" Years later, I understood that the choir was actually saying, "I need thee, Oh, I need thee."

I attended a Pentecostal church, and at age fifteen, I enrolled into a Catholic high school. I grew up in various rule-oriented environments. My mom was a schoolteacher, and my dad was a judge. After graduation, I attended the

United States Military Academy. At West Point, we adhered to lots of rules. When we fell short, we'd have to "Walk the Area." This disciplinary tradition required cadets to pace 120 yards back and forth for hours. One of my friends walked for a total of 345 hours over the course of four years! Typically, every cadet would walk at least one hour over their four-year college experience. I humbly confess that I never had to walk a single hour. In West Point vernacular, I was a "tool"—a functional instrument that followed the rules without fail. This was hardly a surprise given my upbringing.

For years, it was easy for me to focus on adhering to Scripture and applying what I learned in church. Yet, there was a thirst within me that wasn't quenched by my rule-based performance. Reading the Bible wasn't enough. Attending church wasn't enough. Giving my tithe wasn't enough. There was a yearning for more of God that wasn't satisfied by my daily Christian routine. I was unsatisfied merely living *for* God.

There is an interesting story about a group of military commanders in World War II. They were faced with the dilemma of improving aircraft durability; too many U.S. planes were getting shot down.[ii] The officers decided to reinforce the armor around the wings and fuselage because these areas consistently sustained the most damage *amongst the returning aircraft*. One man dissented. He was not a military officer; he was a mathematician. Abraham Wald came to a different conclusion. He recommended reinforcing the tailpiece and the cockpit. You see, *amongst the planes that didn't return*, this is where the damage occurred.[iii] The military commanders had similar roles, training, and experiences, which led them to a similar conclusion. But a divergent view resulted in added value.

I am not a theologian or a pastor, and I don't profess to be an Abraham Wald. My perspective more closely resembles that of Rahab, a prostitute who noticed what the Lord was doing, despite her occupation. Or Peter, a fisherman whose wisdom was a product of God's grace and His Spirit. But I would surmise that I can, most likely, be equated with the ass that Balaam rode, nearly to his death (Numbers 22 ASV). Three times Balaam rode toward the angel's sword, but each time the donkey avoided the conflict. Beaten by the hand of Balaam, alas, the donkey spoke, because God allowed it. *Ve i donkeime, ni quet-.*[iv]

Today, fewer people are attending organized church services.[vvi] For many believers, there is a void in living a life *for* God in a way that *almost* reflects His nature. *Almost falls short.* I wrote this book for readers, like myself, who live with the relentless thought that God is drawing them closer. I believe the Lord is inviting us to live *with* Him and experience more of His divine nature.

# INTRODUCTION

## WHERE IS JESUS?

Joseph and Mary and their kids journeyed to Jerusalem to attend the annual festival of the Passover. Like Christmas or Easter, the Feast of the Passover was a sacred occasion. There was singing and dancing, oratory expositions, and dedications. It was seven days of commemoration, unleavened bread, and thanksgiving. Observed for centuries, even practiced by Moses and King David, the Feast of the Passover honored the power and presence of God. After a week of God-centered merriment, Joseph and Mary begin their journey home. While reminiscing among family and friends, something isn't quite right: Someone is absent. A day passes, and the awkward moment returns; there is a noticeable silence. Although they haven't seen Him in a while, they think Jesus is in their company. The Scriptures tell us that the couple begins to look for Him. "Hey, have you seen Jesus?" "Excuse me, have you seen Jesus since the festival?" The frightening possibility that Jesus has been left by His parents turns into a harsh reality. Despite their love for Him, the couple inadvertently left Jesus. This wouldn't be the last time loving and devoted people would leave Jesus behind.

Joseph and Mary spend the next three days frantically retracing their steps to find their adolescent son. As they return to Jerusalem, they face anxiety, worry, maybe even blame. "He was with you." "Yeah, but you said we were ready to leave." Periods of silence and restlessness as they wonder, "Why didn't our Son follow us home? Where has He been sleeping? What has He been doing? Is He okay?" Their search and rescue lead them to a Jerusalem synagogue. Pushing open the doors, with hearts full of hope, they discover a crowd in awe of a pre-teenage boy. Unlike His contemporaries, Jesus spent three days among the religious elite sitting, listening, and asking questions. And "all who heard him were amazed at his understanding and his answers" (Luke 2:47).

I can only imagine the look on Joseph's and Mary's faces when their eyes catch His. The exhausted parents are relieved but bewildered. Their questions remain, "Has He been here the past three days? Why are people looking at my Son with that awestruck glance? How does He know the answers to these questions?" Despite the supernatural circumstances, Mary's response is quite natural. Mary approaches Jesus and says, "Son...why have you done this to us? Your father and I have been frantic, searching for you everywhere" (Luke 2:48). And at that moment, young Divinity looks into the eyes of parental humanity and says, "But why did you need to search?...Didn't you know that I must be in my Father's house?" (Luke 2:49). Jesus' parents fail to understand His explanation, but Mary keeps these things within her heart. Despite twelve years of observing Jesus' first stumbles, steps, words, and wonders, these loving parents fail to recognize His true nature. As a result, while Christ was in the center of His Father's will, He was left behind by His parents. How did Mary and Joseph lose their immaculately conceived Son and find themselves stumbling at His divine nature?

# LAW-ABIDING CITIZEN

Shortly after Jesus reprimanded His disciples for their attempts to protect Him from children and infants, a young man desperately approaches. He runs up to Jesus and kneels before Him, asking, "Good Teacher, what good thing shall I do that I may have eternal life?" (Matthew 19:16 NKJV). Jesus, downplaying his use of the term "good," advises him to "keep the commandments" (Matt. 19:17 NKJV). Specifically, don't murder, sleep with another man's wife, steal, or be a false witness; and do honor your parents and love your neighbor. The young man responds, "All these things I have kept from my youth. What do I still lack?" (Matt. 19:20 NKJV). This youthful seeker was a proficient rule follower. Not only had he resisted any urge to murder, steal, or commit adultery, despite his youth, he honored his parents and loved his neighbors. Nonetheless, he recognized a void, and so did Jesus.

"What do I still lack?" the young man asks. "Then Jesus, looking at him, loved him" (Mark 10:21 NKJV). That phrase is worth a pause. Jesus acknowledges the enthusiastic pursuer by looking at him. It was more than a glimpse. A connection occurred. A gaze so authentic that the apostle Mark recognized Jesus' love for this seeker. The young man waits for Jesus' response. Jesus answers, "One thing you lack: Go your way, sell whatever you have and give to the poor, and you will have treasure in heaven; and come, take up the cross, and follow Me" (Mark 10:21 NKJV). Jesus' first response regarding the commandments was general, but this response is specific, and it renders the young man speechless. Jesus directs him to let go of the things he personally values and to come and follow Him. When the young man hears Jesus' invitation, he grows sorrowful and walks away. How did a young man committed to obeying the commandments and pursuing God find himself walking *away from* Jesus?

## LEAVING JESUS BEHIND

Both of these stories begin with people living godly lifestyles. They exhibited hearts inclined toward God. Jesus' parents were returning from the feast of the Passover. As one of the most sacred Jewish holidays, it served as a remembrance of God using His miraculous power to free His people. As a family, Joseph and Mary were participating in the festival named after the tenth and final plague, in which God killed the Egyptian firstborns while "passing over" the Israelite firstborns.

Independent of his riches, the young man sought Jesus. Irrespective of his stature, he publicly ran and knelt before Jesus. This gentleman had been keeping the commandments since his youth. This wasn't an event; it was a lifestyle. In the case of Jesus' parents and the young proselyte, despite their godly lifestyles, they found themselves *without* Jesus.

In each case, they demonstrated a comfort with following commandments, but somehow their duty fell short. Mary and Joseph committed the time and resources to travel to Jerusalem. Jesus' parents gladly obeyed the commandment regarding Passover attendance (Numbers 9:12-13) by taking the time to honor God for His miraculous deliverance. They recognized God's authority by participating in the pilgrimage every year. Their traditions and customs were consistent with a godly life. But when Jesus' actions departed from their expectations, they discovered they were no longer *with* Him.

Interestingly, the young man's riches did not get in the way of him keeping the commandments, but they did get in the way of Jesus' invitation. The man was able to follow all of the commandments from his youth, despite his riches. He was comfortable with an ordered and logical approach to living *for* God, an approach based on conditionality and obedience to gain eternal life. From the beginning of his interaction with Jesus, he subjugated himself. The idea of hierarchy and following rules to please authority were acceptable. But letting go of the things he valued to follow Jesus was met with sorrow and rejection.

As he walks away, Jesus shares how difficult it is for the rich to enter into the kingdom of heaven. It's hard for us to take the hand of Jesus when we are clasping something else, even seemingly godly beliefs and convictions. Upon hearing this, Jesus' disciples reply, "Then who in the world can be saved?" (Matt. 19:25). And Jesus says, "Humanly speaking, it is impossible. But *WITH GOD* everything is possible" (Matt. 19:26, emphasis mine). Jesus is introducing His parents and pursuer to an aspect of His nature that goes beyond living *for* Him. He invites them into the unabridged life of living *with* Him.

## A MODEL OF DIVINE NATURE

*Almost* explores the reality of people leaving Jesus behind out of a misunderstanding of His divine nature. It's sobering to think about how often people who loved Jesus misinterpreted, misread, misidentified, and misjudged Him. And we continue to *miss* Him today. Like Mary and Joseph, we become distracted by our expectations and find ourselves walking in Christendom but no longer walking *with* the Lord. Or similar to the young ruler, we press to get closer to God by intensifying our scriptural adherence, but something is still lacking. Despite our performance, we feel a void. There is a fulfillment in our relationship *with* Jesus that goes beyond adherence. To experience Jesus more fully, we must be willing to grab hold of His nature. The apostle Peter wrote,

> May God give you more and more grace and peace as you grow in your knowledge of God and Jesus our Lord. By his divine power, God has given us everything we need for living a godly life. We have received all of this by coming to **know him**, the one who called us to himself by means of his marvelous glory and excellence. And because of his glory and excellence, he has given us great and precious promises. These are the promises that enable you to **share his divine nature** and escape the world's corruption caused by human desires. (2 Peter 1:2-4, emphasis mine)

We were designed to know Him and to share His nature.

I created a framework to explore God's divine nature. The X-axis is based on two divine roles that appear throughout the Scriptures. They are the Commander and Companion roles. The Lord's role as Commander is illustrated in an unsuspecting visit. On a trip back from Capernaum, a Roman officer approached Jesus. The soldier came and begged Jesus to heal his bed-stricken servant. Jesus agreed to go to the officer's house to heal the ailing helper, but the Roman soldier refused to let Jesus enter his home. The officer said, "Lord, I am not worthy to have you come into my home. Just say the word from where you are, and my servant will be healed. I know this because I am under the authority of my superior officers, and I have authority over my soldiers. I only need to say, 'Go,' and they go, or 'Come,' and they come. And if I say to my slaves, 'Do this,' they do it" (Matthew 8:8-9). Jesus was pleasantly surprised by the officer's faith and ordered the healing of his servant. I labeled this role Commander because it exemplifies the authoritative nature of Divinity. The Roman soldier acknowledged Jesus as the Commander. He understood that sickness was under Jesus' command, and all Jesus had to do was give the order, and his servant would be made whole.

It was a summer day in New Jersey when I was unmistakably introduced to the role of commander. A couple of weeks earlier, I had graduated from high school. I was reporting to my first day as a cadet at the United States Military Academy Preparatory School in Fort Dix, New Jersey. The day began on a joyous note, as about 150 incoming cadets took an oath to protect and defend the constitution in front of celebrating friends and families. But the celebration was quickly disrupted as drill sergeants entered the auditorium and directed us out. There was no question who was in charge and who wasn't, as my hairstyle, speech, walk, clothing, and individual rights were summarily changed.

In this role of Commander, the Lord is mission-focused. His behavior is ordered and logical. In Genesis, the world begins mysteriously, and we are introduced to God's Commanding nature. He orders form to a formless world. He fills an empty world with plants, animals, and humanity. To a darkened world, He commands light. He fixes problems!

Through His Commanding nature, conditionality and cause and effect are established, as He creates processes like seed-time, and harvest. Our relationship with the Lord, as Commander, resembles the relationship between a king and his servants, protocoled and formal. Our communication with Him primarily is characterized by His directives and commands. Like soldiers, individual choice is largely constrained as we exercise restraint and conformity. The Commander is pleased through obedience to His universal directives.

The other role we see throughout Scripture is the role of Companion. The other day, I met with a friend, and he was reminiscing about when he was in college, young and in love. His love interest was also in college about three and a half hours away. We laughed as he shared that he spent more time traveling to see her than actually being with her. Despite the distance, he would faithfully visit. And after each short weekend visit and seven hours of driving, he would look forward to seeing her again. It didn't make sense, but it didn't have to *because he was in love.*

The Companion role is cast in unconditionality as God exemplifies undeserved grace and agape love, without reason or cause. As Companion, the Lord's focus is directed more to people than being mission-oriented. As a result, behavior is less ordered and may appear incongruent and depart from human reasoning. The relationship is less hierarchal and more collaborative, resembling the connection between a bridegroom and a bride. Questions and dialogue characterize the nature of communication. And choice is less constrained, allowing for free will. Ultimately, in the role of Companion, Divinity is pleased through our responses to personal and specific instructions, which may deviate from established norms.

The Y-axis is based on earthly or heavenly outcomes. Earthly outcomes pertain to this world, our present desires, and requirements. Jesus' physical location was of earthly interest to His parents. Scriptural examples of earthly outcomes include physical healings (Matt. 8:1-4), financial blessings (Matt. 17:27), provision (John 2:1-11), freedom from demonic oppression (Matt. 8:16), etc. Heavenly outcomes are matters pertaining to the world to come. The rich young ruler was interested in eternal life, a heavenly outcome. Other heavenly outcomes include redemption (Galatians 2:20), the crown of life (James 1:12), and salvation (Luke 23:43), etc.

The combination of the X- and Y-axes results in a 2x2 framework of The Four Blends of Divine Nature®: Earthly Commander, Heavenly Commander, Earthly Companion, and Heavenly Companion. Two of these blends are authoritative, while the other two are participative. The framework consists of four equally essential blends of God's nature. Frames help us to recognize patterns more quickly, identify aspects we would generally miss, and ultimately gain a better understanding. This framework isn't perfect, but exploring each blend allows us to have a more holistic view of our Creator. Studying each combination independently will enable us to have a more comprehensive view of our Creator.

These revelations lead us to interact with the Lord as servant AND friend, as soldier AND bride.

# THIS BOOK'S JOURNEY

The moon is a reflective surface with no light of its own; like a mirror, it merely reflects the sun. But if a mirror has a distorted view of an image, it will produce a contorted reflection. God created us in His image, and we were designed to reflect His nature. But a distorted view of His nature results in a contorted image, preventing us from reflecting His glory (2 Corinthians 3:18). This book examines the progression of growing beyond the scripted life of living *for* God to living *with* God. By scripted life, I mean a life that primarily seeks to coincide with Judeo-Christian norms (church attendance, Bible reading, serving the community, etc.). The goal is to exchange it for a life characterized by an interactive connection *with* our Creator in a uniquely original way. Living *for* God get us close to God, like a golf ball sitting on the edge. But the game's objective isn't to get the ball *almost* in the hole. The goal of this book is two-fold. It's to answer the question: am I leaving God behind by living *for* Him, at the expense of His nature? And it's to awaken the author and readers alike to having the dynamic, personal relationship we were designed to have *with* a personal and intimate God.

To explore this, we will examine each of The Four Blends of Divine Nature® independently. We will describe and summarize each blend. We will explore scriptural examples, examine the results of each blend, and discuss the implications on our lives today. We'll explore how experiencing or performing godly miracles may still leave us eternally separated. We'll examine how abandonment is a necessary part of our Christ-like transformation. We'll discover how Jesus' unique response to a woman caught having illicit sex teaches us something about intimacy. We will visit common Christian practices, like prayer, worship, and *What Would Jesus Do?*, and see if they are drawing us closer or pushing us further from God. I hope you'll join me in this pursuit.

# CHAPTER I

# FIRST BLEND: EARTHLY COMMANDER

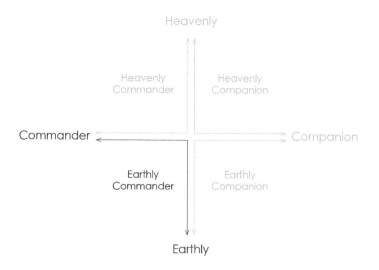

## A DESPERATE FATHER

Jesus, Peter, James, and John return from a secluded mountain getaway. As they draw near, they see the other disciples arguing with the religious elite in the middle of a crowd. So much for peace and quiet. The crowd is excited to see Jesus, and they run to meet Him. Jesus asks the multitude, "What is all this arguing about?" (Mark 9:16). A father speaks up, "Teacher, I brought my son so you could heal him" (Mark 9:17). He was the dad of a tortured boy. In Jesus' absence, the father had approached His disciples, seeking peace for his son. His child couldn't speak. He experienced intermittent convulsions. Time and time again, his boy was tossed to the ground with no relief. His son was distressed continually by a tormenting spirit.

The father came pleading on his son's behalf, but Jesus' disciples failed to take authority over the spirit. Jesus is not amused. He reprimands them in verse 19, "You faithless people! How long must I be with you? How long must I put up with you?" Jesus' rebuke is direct. "Bring the boy to me," He orders (v. 19). There is no question who is in charge. The crowd obeys. As they bring the boy toward Jesus, the dark spirit revolts. It flings the boy, causing him to writhe in pain and foam at the mouth. This was the spirit's customary treatment. Jesus inquires how long this had been happening. The father replies, "Since he was a little boy. The spirit often throws him into the fire or into water, trying to kill him. Have mercy on us and help us, if you can" (Mark 9:21-22).

Jesus doesn't miss the desperate father's wavering tone. "'What do you mean, "If I can"?' Jesus asked. 'Anything is possible if a person believes'" (Mark 9:23). After sleepless nights of hearing his son being thrown about recklessly, after years of his son's seemingly suicidal tendencies, and after a failed rescue at the hands of Jesus' disciples, this father cries out. "Lord, I believe; help my unbelief!" (Mark 9:24 NKJV). Jesus speaks, "Listen, you spirit that makes this boy unable to hear and speak...I command you to come out of this child and never enter him again!" (Mark 9:25). Jesus commands the spirit to leave, and it leaves, impacting the son's condition and his father's heart immediately.

# EARTHLY COMMANDER NATURE EXPLAINED

As Earthly Commander, the Lord operates in His authority to meet our present circumstances. This blend is goal-centric. It's logical and structured, with outcomes that influence our earthly circumstances. The performance of miracles is indicative of this blend. This story is no exception, beginning with a father in need of someone to change his son's earthly condition. In Jesus' absence, he brought his son to Jesus' disciples, but they failed to cast out the spirit, although they had cast out spirits previously (Mark 6:13). An argument ensued.

When Jesus returns, He establishes order. Given Jesus' reputation for healing the sick, it was logical that this father would seek Him. Upon hearing about the situation, Jesus orders the boy forward. Jesus' nature is formal, as He directs the crowd, chastises His disciples, and sternly questions the father for doubting His authority. The father capitulates, immediately addressing Jesus as Lord and asking for help even related to his unbelief. And the story concludes as the disciples, the crowd, the father, and the spirit all respond to Jesus in complete obedience.

This blend focuses on attaining our earthly needs from God. It applies practical actions to achieve present-world objectives. Behaviorally, it consists of following commands to impact current conditions. In this perspective, the proximity between God and man is like a king and a servant. God's authority limits our actions, as we meet conditions in order to achieve an outcome. Pleasing God, in this blend, is achieved through obedience. The Old and New Testaments reflect God's Earthly Commander nature. It's evident when God visits King Solomon and says,

> "At times I might shut up the heavens so that no rain falls, or command grasshoppers to devour your crops, or send plagues among you. Then if my people who are called by my name will humble themselves and pray and seek my face and turn from their wicked ways, I will hear from heaven and will forgive their sins and restore their land." (2 Chronicles 7:13-14)

At times, God may command negative consequences. But if His people meet the expected conditions (humility, prayer, seek, turn), as Commander, He will allow a different earthly outcome (healing the land). This is an example of conditional adherence to influence earthly circumstances.

Contemplate an offertory example:

"You are under a curse, for your whole nation has been cheating me. Bring all the tithes into the storehouse so there will be enough food in my Temple. If you do," says the Lord of Heaven's Armies, "I will open the windows of heaven for you. I will pour out a blessing so great you won't have enough room to take it in! Try it! Put me to the test!" (Malachi 3:9-10)

Here, the condition is "bring the tithe," and the Commander will direct an earthly outcome—a blessing. Alternatively, if we fail to bring the tithe, the Lord will order a different earthly outcome—a curse.

A New Testament example is the principle of seedtime and harvest. In writing to the Corinthians, Paul said, "Remember this—a farmer who plants only a few seeds will get a small crop. But the one who plants generously will get a generous crop" (2 Cor. 9:6). It is conditional, logical, and ordered. The harvest is dependent upon the sowing of seed. Paul provided another example when reasoning with the Thessalonians: "Even while we were with you, we gave you this command: 'Those unwilling to work will not get to eat'" (2 Thess. 3:10).

This blend is known as the **Awareness** Response. Our reaction to the Lord's Earthly Commander nature is often an increased awareness of Him. As an example, the father and the crowd became aware of Jesus' ability to heal, so they brought the mute child to Him. The word aware means

"having or showing realization, perception, or knowledge."
[vii]In this blend, we realize, perceive, or gain knowledge regarding the reality of God and His ability to meet our needs. Upon Jesus telling the woman at the well the specifics regarding her marital status, she replied, "Sir, I perceive that You are a prophet" (John 4:19 NKJV). She realized or came into the knowledge of Jesus. God's Earthly Commander nature often serves as our introduction to God. The table below characteristically summarizes the Awareness Response.

### 7 Characteristics of the Awareness Response

| | |
|---:|---|
| *Focus* | Earthly needs |
| *Context* | A logical approach to present circumstances |
| *Roles* | King/Servant |
| *Communication* | Current concerns met by following commands |
| *Proximity* | Formal |
| *Choice* | Restricting choice to affect current conditions |
| *Pleasing God* | Obeying directives & meeting conditions |

# PRODUCTIVITY AND BELIEF

The Earthly Commander nature aims to **produce**. It is the performance of behaviors to produce a desired earthly outcome, like healings, finances, provision, etc. In our focus on Christ to produce, the act of giving could be expressed as "giving to receive." As exemplified in Jesus' interaction with the tormented boy, through God's authoritative nature, we achieve earthly outcomes by adhering to directives and commands. We live quid pro quo. This blend is often a starting place as God's Earthly Commander nature generates the opportunity to ignite *belief.* This chapter began with a desperate father who believed enough to seek out Jesus. Following the failed attempts of Jesus' disciples and the spirit throwing his son down as he was approaching Jesus, the father's belief wavered. But in response to Jesus' authoritative tone, the father's faith was ignited…"Lord, I believe…"

Consider Jesus' miracle in Cana of Galilee. Jesus and the disciples are hanging out at a wedding when they run out of wine. It seems a far cry from a father pleading on behalf of his haunted son. Nonetheless, Mary requisitions Jesus to help with this inventory problem. Leaving Jesus behind in the temple is one thing, but leveraging your Son's incarnate powers for a beer run is another. You have to love the Scriptures. Here, we learn something special about Jesus, and His availability to discuss all our cares. Jesus responds like it's a bad idea, "Dear woman, that's not our problem…My time has not yet come" (John 2:4). Although you have to be nice to your mom, Jesus' response was similar to when His parents cornered Him in the Jerusalem synagogue. Jesus was here for a purpose, and it was more than ensuring the wine didn't run out. But Mary ignores her Son's resistance and instructs the wedding servants to do whatever Jesus tells them to do. Jesus proceeds with the directives "fill," "dip," and "take," and the servants obey. The wine is great, the party continues, but most importantly, "his disciples **believed** in him" (John 2:11, emphasis mine). Jesus performed many miracles to meet earthly needs, and by producing "many **believed** in His name when they saw the signs which He did" (John 2:23 NKJV, emphasis mine).

This theme is consistent in the Old and New Testaments. God met human needs, often through the miraculous, to build belief in His people. Remember the Passover, God supernaturally delivering Israel out of the hands of the Egyptians. God said to Moses, "When I raise my powerful hand and bring out the Israelites, the Egyptians will know that I am the Lord" (Exodus 7:5). This deliverance was an unforgettable introduction. In telling Moses what to say to Pharaoh, God said, "'I will show you that I am the Lord.' Look! I will strike the water of the Nile with this staff in my hand, and the river will turn to blood" (Ex. 7:17). Once again, He produced miracles to meet the dire needs of His chosen people. Ponder Jesus' retort to the religious elite, "Don't believe me unless I carry out my Father's work. But if I do his work, **believe in the evidence of the miraculous works I have done, even if you don't believe me**. Then you will know and understand that the Father is in me, and I am in the Father" (John 10:37-38, emphasis mine).

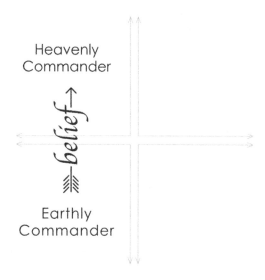

Heavenly
Commander

Earthly
Commander

Our relationship with Christ often begins with Him addressing our most troubling concerns. As our Creator resolves them, our trust in Him increases. Isn't this also true of us? As we make good on our promises to our spouse, children, coworkers, etc., we discover that their belief in us increases. In response to Jesus' fruitfulness, we have the opportunity to believe in Him. Few things endear trust like hope fulfilled, whether that need is a healing, a way out, a bill, or another glass of wine. For this reason, productivity is often foundational to belief, but it's intended to be a starting place, not a destination. What were the surrounding circumstances when you became aware of God? What circumstances led you to believe?

# LOSING GOD IN THE BLESSINGS

The Earthly Commander perspective is clearly scriptural. Still, it's limited by our tendency to prioritize our earthly needs over God's will. As we focus on fulfilling conditions to meet earthly provisions, we can lose sight of God. This is evident in the following testimony. Battling sickness for almost four decades, a lame man consistently fought through a crowd of blind, sick, and injured people. Every so often, an angel would come and trouble the water of this Bethesda pool. And the first person to enter the water following this angelic disruption was healed from their affliction. First Naaman in the Jordan, then a blind man at the Pool of Siloam, experienced healing waters.

Now, a lame man at this Bethesda pool sought aqua therapy persistently. Being first was the condition that would lead to his new life. He'd no longer have to battle the crowd. No longer would his days focus on positioning. He'd finally be done with this pool. If he could only be first, a new life lay ahead, a sentiment familiar to many of us. When Jesus asks him if he would like to get well, the man responds, "I can't, sir…for I have no one to put me into the pool when the water bubbles up. Someone else always gets there ahead of me" (John 5:7). Understandably so, he is so focused on pursuing the miracle that he loses sight of the miracle worker. He focuses on fulfilling specific conditions to meet his earthly need. If I can be first in the pool (condition), then I can get healed (outcome). But he is blind to the fact that he is speaking with the One who can stir the water. He wasn't the only one to make this mistake.

Following the disciples' successful outing casting out demons and curing diseases, Jesus departs on another team retreat, this time with all of the disciples. A crowd catches a glimpse of Him leaving by boat and recognizes Him. Like a throng of paparazzi, despite being ill-prepared, they give chase. They catch up with Him in unincorporated Bethsaida. Did this crowd perform an impromptu 5K in pursuit of Jesus? Their commitment moves the Lord. He teaches the group about the kingdom of God. He heals them. Some of the disciples are forward-thinking. Given the time of day, size of the crowd, the journey there, the lack of funds and food, the disciples recommend sending the group away to eat. It is a reasonable suggestion, but Jesus challenges them to provide for the crowd, saying, "They do not need to go away. You give them something to eat" (Matt. 14:16 NKJV). Despite their recent success in healing others, the disciples, like the injured man laying poolside, focus on the condition and lose sight of the Commander. They respond to Jesus by saying, "Shall we go and buy two hundred denarii worth of bread and give them something to eat?" (Mark 6:37 NKJV). They suffered from a need-based focus. But Jesus, not restricted by conditions, once again produces to meet the earthly need.

Jesus miraculously feeds the crowd, and they love it! But their love for Jesus became *conditional*.

Jesus' blessing over the five-loaves-two-fish family pack left quite an impression. The Scriptures read, "When the people saw him do this miraculous sign, they exclaimed, 'Surely, he is the Prophet we have been expecting!'" (John 6:14). The crowd's reaction is understandable; Jesus just fed more than five thousand with a two-piece dinner. Plus, there were leftovers! With Him as their king, they'd never want for food again. But the crowd loses sight of Jesus by focusing on their yearnings. They decide to make Jesus their king, independent of His purpose. Earthly kingship was never Jesus' pursuit; nonetheless, the crowd prioritizes its daily sustenance over Jesus' heavenly call. Their reaction forces Jesus to leave. "When Jesus saw that they were ready to force him to be their king, he slipped away into the hills by himself" (John 6:15). An Earthly Commander context maintains some semblance of distance. Although outwardly they are pursuing Him, inwardly they are pursuing their own desires.

The crowd becomes focused on Jesus' ability to provide. Jesus flees by boat, and the crowd follows Him to Capernaum (John 6:24-25). It appears the people love Jesus and want to make Him their king, but Jesus exposes their ambitions. He says, "I tell you the truth, you want to be with me because I fed you, not because you understood the miraculous signs" (John 6:26). They did not pursue Jesus out of belief, but for relief. Like a fickle band of freeloaders, they pursued Jesus because they wanted to be fed, contin-

ually. What irony. When this crowd initially sought ⅃˛
He taught, healed, and fed them. He was among them. But
when they clamored to make Him king, He responded with
distance and separation. The injured man, the disciples, and
the crowd all lost sight of Jesus by focusing on their desires,
and so do we.

# THE GMAT

I grew up in the '80s watching *Family Ties*. Michael J.
Fox played the role of Alex P. Keaton, the entrepreneurial
son. He was my favorite character. Throughout elementa-
ry school, I won numerous fundraisers selling cookies and
chocolate assortments to my friends' parents and my parents' friends. Unbeknownst to them, they were on a month-
ly subscription. I was always selling something. When I entered high school, I took every business course and won the
Business Achievement Award. After attending West Point
and serving in the Army, I dreamed of going back to school
and earning my master's in business administration (MBA).
But there was one obstacle, the Graduate Management Ad-
missions Test (affectionately known as the GMAT). I was a
notoriously poor scholastic test taker. The combination of
bringing a photo ID, a No. 2 pencil, and a Scantron (ma-
chine-readable answer sheet) somehow brought out the
worst in me. Sure, I attended West Point, but let's just say I
took the SAT more than once. But surely this test would be

different. I thought to myself, "I graduated from West Point. I was an Army officer. I can defeat a scholastic test." And with that, Operation Overcome began.

Like the lame man sitting at the brink of his deliverance, my mission was clear. Be first. Or in this case, perform well on the GMAT to attend business school. Similar to the disciples surveying the hungry crowd, I assessed the situation. I conceded I was not a good test taker. No problem—I employed the assistance of one of the best educational service companies in the country. For six months, I drove 270 miles to GMAT classes twice a week with my wife and our fifteen-month-old son. It's worth mentioning that my wife was pregnant with our daughter at the time. It was a three-hour drive one way! From January to June, I studied at least twenty hours per week. I took the practice GMAT at least forty times, with great success. Commitment plus training plus repetition leads to results, *right?* I was ready! I officially took the GMAT for the first time in the early summer. I arrived with my photo ID. A computer station had replaced the dreadful No. 2 pencil and its ghastly accomplice, the Scantron form. I welcomed the new format.

As I progressed through the test, I could feel the anxiety coming over me. I was trying to keep my calm and work my way into it. But something was wrong. An interesting feature of the GMAT is that it's a computerized adaptive test. If the test taker is performing well, the difficulty level of the questions grows harder. Contrastingly, if the test taker is performing poorly, the difficulty of the problems becomes easier. By the end of my test, the computer was mocking me with $x+3=7$. Despite driving 500 miles a week and studying more than 500 hours, my digital experience was just another Scantron. Operation Overcome was a failure. But like the recently fed crowd, I was persistent. I enlisted in another six weeks of training, retook the GMAT, and failed again! I was distraught and gave up on my ambition to attend business school.

Shortly after that, we moved to Atlanta, Georgia. I transitioned from my Army career and began civilian life working as a sales representative for Johnson and Johnson. I loved my job. I had the opportunity to work with surgeons and assist them in improving patient care. Outside of work, I enjoyed reading non-fiction business hardbacks. I loved everything about the subject, and my desire to attend business school quietly reignited. I researched what evening MBA programs were available in Atlanta, and I fell in love with the Goizueta Business School at Emory University...but what about the GMAT? I winced at the memory. Then one day, my wife said, "Babe, you should apply. You have no idea what the Lord may do. Just apply." I listened to her and applied. Shortly after that, Emory accepted me into the program! Surprisingly, as a military officer with an undergrad technical degree, working in a technical field, I was eligible for a GMAT waiver. Who knew? God knew! I spent years and thousands of dollars focusing on meeting a specific condition, and then God provided independent of my performance. And I learned to trust Him more.

Many of us excessively prioritize this Awareness Response. We focus on improving our present situations through conditional performance. We focus more on Jesus' response to our wishes than us responding to Jesus. We become overly focused on His productivity, giving tithes to "eat of the loaves and be filled." At times, our prayers are dominated by requests. We ask for healing, financial blessing, jobs, getting out of debt, improving our marriages, and other present desires. These requests are not bad things to pray for. Peter reminds us to "Give all your worries and cares to God, for he cares about you" (1 Peter 5:7). But our cares should never dominate our focus. Like the lame man at the edge of the pool, we believe our situation can change if we can just *be first*. We strive to receive, personifying the seemingly committed crowd, as we make Jesus our genie, serving Him only as a means to a granted wish.

But what happens when we are not interested in believing in Him but only in receiving from Him? We become set in interacting with God's divine nature solely to have our earthly circumstances influenced. Like the crowd filled by Jesus' miraculous loaves, we mistakenly rest in the miracles when the purpose of productivity is belief. Remember, Jesus only fed the hungry crowd once. They sought Him not because they saw Him perform the miraculous and believed; they sought Him because they ate and were filled, temporarily. But that is not the intention of God's Earthly Commander nature. The intention is belief, which gives us reason to change how we live; it is the impetus to trusting God to meet our eternal needs as we conform to His image.

This progression of belief is an important part of the maturation of our relationship with Christ. Our lack of belief is an indication that we don't *know* Him, or it's an indication that we don't care to know Him. Scripturally, we can see the damaging effects of unbelief. Consider Jesus' experience when He returned to His hometown. No longer the boy who grew up whittling wood in Joseph's shop, "he began teaching in the synagogue, and many who heard him were amazed. They asked, 'Where did he get all this wisdom and the power to perform such miracles?' Then they scoffed, 'He's just a carpenter, the son of Mary and the brother of James, Joseph, Judas, and Simon. And his sisters live right here among us.' They were deeply offended and refused to believe in him" (Mark 6:2-3).

The hometown crowd couldn't reconcile Jesus' present with Jesus' past. They couldn't see Jesus as a teacher because they were too distracted by their memory of Him as a carpenter and Mary's boy. And the dissonance between Jesus' outward similarities but inward differences drove them to offense. They saw Jesus operating in His purpose. Although they were astonished, they were *offended,* and their offense gave way to unbelief. The gospel of Mark shares, "And because of their unbelief, he couldn't do any miracles among them except to place his hands on a few sick people and heal them. And he was amazed at their unbelief" (Mark 6:5-6).

Unbelief debilitates our relationship with God because it communicates, "I don't believe You or I don't believe in You." And unbelief is a persistent challenge in the relationship between God and us. Even after Jesus came back from the dead, He rebuked His disciples "for their stubborn unbelief because they refused to believe those who had seen him after he had been raised from the dead" (Mark 16:14). But God's earthly fruitfulness leads us into belief, and that belief supports us in conforming to His image.

Eventually, this strategy of pursuing God only to fulfill our earthly desires results in us finding ourselves absent from His presence. It wasn't a bad idea for the crowd to eat, but we never see Jesus feeding this crowd again. Distance and separation followed their ill-advised, yet committed, efforts. Our pursuits for productivity, to the exclusion of the Producer, leave us unproductive. We must learn how to have a more balanced approach. Earthly Commander is only one of four blends. Paul illustrated a different perspective, "Yet what we suffer now is nothing compared to the glory he will reveal to us later" (Romans 8:18). He elected to focus beyond this earthly realm into something a bit more heavenly.

# RECAP

- The Earthly Commander, also known as the Awareness Response, often serves as our introduction to God. We become aware of Him in the context of meeting our needs and the needs of others.

- This blend is logical and structured, with outcomes that influence our earthly circumstances.

- Through the fulfillment of specific directives or commands, desired earthly outcomes are achieved (i.e., seed-time and harvest).

- The outcome of God's Earthly Commander nature is productivity.

- The crowd attempted to forcibly make Jesus their earthly king, prioritizing their desire above Jesus' purpose.

- We must be careful not to prioritize our earthly needs over God's will.

- Be cautious: as we focus on fulfilling conditions to meet earthly provisions, we can lose sight of God.

- Key biblical stories: Man at the pool (John 5), water to wine (John 2), and Jesus feeds the 5,000 (John 6)

# CHAPTER 2

# SECOND BLEND: HEAVENLY COMMANDER

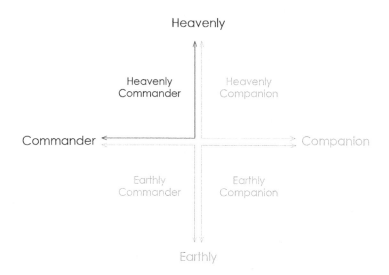

Heavenly

Heavenly
Commander

Heavenly
Companion

Commander ← — — — — — — — → Companion

Earthly
Commander

Earthly
Companion

Earthly

## A FRIGHTFUL JAILER

Paul and Silas were staying at the home of Lydia, a recent convert known for her high-priced fabric. On their way to prayer, they are disturbed by a fortune-telling girl. Influenced by a wicked spirit, she follows behind Paul and Silas, yelling, "These men are servants of the Most High God, and they have come to tell you how to be saved" (Acts 16:17). This goes on for days. Eventually, Paul has had enough. He exhaustedly turns to the girl and casts out the annoying spirit. Peace and quiet ensue, but the slave girl's lucrative fortune-telling ability is revoked. Her owners are enraged. They drag Paul and Silas to the city officials and make false accusations against them. The duo is publicly stripped, beaten, and thrown into prison. The jailer is ordered to make sure these profit-squelching meddlers do not escape.

The jailer responds by putting them in the securest part of the prison, with their ankles fastened. Despite the conditions, Paul and Silas pray and sing to the Lord throughout the night for all to hear. Then, an earthquake shudders the foundations of the prison. It forcefully unlatches the prison doors, and it shakes loose the shackles that kept the incarcerated bound. The jailer awakes. Upon seeing the prison doors open and no prisoners, he assumes the prisoners escaped and prepares to take his own life. A voice cries, "Stop! Don't kill yourself! We are all here!" (Acts 16:28). The jailer pauses and calls for the prison lights.

Strangely, not a single prisoner ran into the night. Paul's and Silas' shackles were opened, but they remain in the innermost parts of the prison. While one might expect the prisoner to run toward freedom, the jailer runs to the imprisoned. No longer concerned about his present responsibilities, the post-suicidal jailer presses his way to the feet of Paul and Silas. He falls before them, and says, "Sirs, what must I do to be saved?" (Acts 16:30). Paul and Silas respond, "Believe in the Lord Jesus and you will be saved, along with everyone in your household" (Acts 16:31).

# HEAVENLY COMMANDER NATURE EXPLAINED

In the Heavenly Commander blend, we see the Lord's authoritative nature related to our condition in the world to come. Our efforts to become *like Jesus* characterize this blend. After experiencing God's miraculous power, we become aware of the reality that there is more to this life than this life. Consequently, we resolve to *adjust* our lives to receive celestial or eternal blessings. The **Adjustment** Response reflects our behavior. Adjust means "to bring to a more satisfactory state" or "to bring the parts of to a true or more effective relative position."[viii] Consider the jailer, after late-night serenades of praise by Paul and Silas, followed by an earthquake that should have led to the great escape. The jailer miraculously finds all the prisoners still present. He responds not by asking, "What must I do to get all of the prison doors latched?" His attention is no longer on his present earthly circumstances as the jailer desperately asks, "Sirs, what must I do to be saved?" (Acts 16:30). Following this traumatic event, he is looking to bring his life into a more satisfactory state.

His questions illustrate a newly birthed willingness to adjust his life to experience salvation. This blend is conditional, but the outcomes pertain to the world to come. In this example, the jailer no longer focuses on the state of the prisoners. His concern has shifted to his family's salvation. The disciples' reply is structured and logical, "Believe in the Lord Jesus and you will be saved, along with everyone in your household" (Acts 16:31). The disciples provide the jailer with a directive that will enable him to achieve his heavenly goal. In this blend, proximity is still formal. Here, the disciples are serving as teachers instructing the jailer along the road to salvation. In formality, the jailer acknowledges the disciples as "Sirs." The relationship between God and man remains hierarchical. This blend is also built on if-then conditionality. If you believe in the Lord Jesus (condition), you will be saved (heavenly outcome).

## 7 Characteristics of the Adjustment Response

| | |
|---|---|
| *Focus* | Eternal life |
| *Context* | A logical approach to the world to come |
| *Roles* | King/Servant or Commander/Soldier celestially |
| *Communication* | Commands directed toward heavenly goals |
| *Proximity* | Formal |
| *Choice* | Restricting choice for eternal reasons |
| *Pleasing God* | Obeying commands to reflect the image of God |

This is evident in other biblical passages, as Paul wrote, "Don't be misled—you cannot mock the justice of God. You will always harvest what you plant. Those who live only to satisfy their own sinful nature will harvest decay and death from that sinful nature. But those who live to please the Spirit will harvest everlasting life from the Spirit" (Galatians 6:7-8). In this example, seedtime and harvest apply again, but the condition is sowing and reaping to the Spirit, and the outcome is everlasting life. Or consider James' directive in James 4:8, "Come close to God" (condition), "and God will come close to you" (heavenly outcome). A conditional statement, but with a heavenly reward. The Beatitudes provide an exhaustive example of this blend, as Jesus said:

> "God blesses those who are poor and realize their need for him,
> for the Kingdom of Heaven is theirs.

God blesses those who mourn,
for they will be comforted.
God blesses those who are humble,
for they will inherit the whole earth.
God blesses those who hunger and thirst for justice,
for they will be satisfied.
God blesses those who are merciful,
for they will be shown mercy.
God blesses those whose hearts are pure,
for they will see God.
God blesses those who work for peace,
for they will be called the children of God.
God blesses those who are persecuted for doing right,
for the Kingdom of Heaven is theirs.
God blesses you when people mock you and persecute you and lie about you and say all sorts of evil things against you because you are my followers. Be happy about it! Be very glad! For a great reward awaits you in heaven. And remember, the ancient prophets were persecuted in the same way." (Matt. 5:3-12)


Each verse presents a condition (i.e., "poor in spirit," "meek," "pure in heart") followed by a future outcome (i.e., "theirs is the kingdom of heaven," "shall inherit the earth," "shall see God"). In Paul's letter to the Romans, he advised them by saying, "If you openly declare with your mouth that Jesus is Lord and believe in your heart that God raised him from the dead, you will be saved" (Rom. 10:9). Salvation begins with a simple ordered rule: confess and believe (action), resulting in forgiveness (outcome).

In the Old Testament, the Lord's instructions to Moses regarding the Sabbath exemplify His Heavenly Commander nature. The preservation of the Sabbath was an acknowledgment of the promise between God and His people. The Lord said, "Tell the people of Israel: 'Be careful to keep my Sabbath day, for the Sabbath is a sign of the covenant between me and you from generation to generation. It is given so you may know that I am the Lord, who makes you holy'" (Ex. 31:12-13). Or consider God's words to Solomon in 2 Chronicles 7:14, "Then if my people who are called by my name will humble themselves and pray and seek my face and turn from their wicked ways" (condition), "I will hear from heaven and will forgive their sins and restore their land" (outcome). The first outcome, forgiveness, is heavenly, while the second, the healing of the land, is earthly.

# CONFORMING TO HIS IMAGE

The Adjustment Response helps us to **conform.** Conformity is defined as "following the rules, standards or laws, compliance upon compliance, or behaving according to socially accepted conventions."[ix] By imitating Christ, we begin to look more like Christ. This is understandable, as authoritative behavior subjects itself to hierarchy. In this case, the relationship resembles that of a soldier and his commander. This dedication helps mold an eighteen-year-old civilian into a soldier, and it also plays a role in helping believers to conform to the image of Christ.

Our growth from Earthly to Heavenly Commander blend involves shifting our focus from earthly to heavenly circumstances. On the strength of our belief, we become interested and willing to adapt our behavior to His. None of this occurs without belief. Conformity without belief is enslavement, but God has never been interested in enlisting slaves. He is interested in assembling friends, joint-heirs, and a bride. He is interested in believers. Matthew records Jesus' final directives to His disciples, "Therefore, go and make disciples of all the nations, baptizing them in the name of the Father and the Son and the Holy Spirit. Teach these new disciples to obey all the commands I have given you. And be sure of this: I am with you always, even to the end of the age" (Matt. 28:19-20). He instructs His disciples to teach the nations to observe everything that He has commanded them to do.

Within this blend, we aim to imitate godly directives. Practically, we apply the Scriptures to our lives. This behavior is consistent with God's promise to us. Peter shared, "For God called you to do good, even if it means suffering, just as Christ suffered for you. He is your example, and you must follow in his steps" (1 Peter 2:21). This is a heavenly, not earthly, conformism. We don't begin to resemble Jesus physically as we follow Scripture, but spiritually. As we obey His commands, we con-form ("con" in Spanish means with) *to* godly standards and Scripture, resulting in Christlikeness. In this Adjustment Response, directives such as "'You must love the Lord your God with all your heart, all your soul, and all your mind'" (Matt. 22:37) or "'Love your neighbor as yourself'" (Matt. 22:39) place our focus on the alignment between God's commands and our performance. We begin to leave behind the relics of our earthly nature and become like Him, heavenly minded.

Paul provoked the Roman, Corinthian, and Philippian churches in this way. To the Romans, he wrote, "For whom He foreknew, He also predestined to be conformed to the image of His Son" (Rom. 8:29 NKJV). In his first letter to the Corinthians, he proclaimed, "And you should imitate me, just as I imitate Christ" (1 Cor. 11:1). And he challenged the Philippians by saying, "You must have the same attitude that Christ Jesus had" (Phil. 2:5). In each case, he encouraged believers to imitate Christ. To look like Christ, we must focus on Christ. But our gaze, like that of a small child, vacillates between our father or mother and our own performance. Conforming to His image causes us to focus on His thoughts, His actions, His deeds, His beliefs, etc., and this is a beautiful thing. In this blend, we give because Christ gave. We serve because Christ served. We love because Christ loved. This blend inspires us *to imitate* Christ. But this can be humbling, as our efforts to obey often fall short.

Our own efforts persistently thwart our conformity. Paul referenced this limitation when he said,

> I want to do what is good, but I don't. I don't want to do what is wrong, but I do it anyway. But if I do what I don't want to do, I am not really the one doing wrong; it is sin living in me that does it.

> I have discovered this principle of life—that when I want to do what is right, I inevitably do what is wrong. I love God's law with all my heart. But there is another power within me that is at war with my mind. This power makes me a slave to the sin that is still within me. (Rom. 7:19-23)

Conformity shows us the limits of our performance, as we struggle to live up to His image while fighting against our sinful nature. Our efforts to imitate Christ are met with frustration, as we fail to do the things God has instructed us to do and are enticed to do those things He has told us not to do. In the context of maturation, these failures are critical as they soften our prideful hearts and open the door for humility.

Our journey with Christ goes beyond our ability to walk to our willingness to get up, again and again and again. Remember, "The godly may trip seven times, but they will get up again. / But one disaster is enough to overthrow the wicked" (Proverbs 24:16). Failure takes us beyond the idea of God to the need for a deeper relationship *with* God. As we pursue conformity, the cycle of falling and getting up teaches us *humility*. It shifts our focus from *our behavior* to *our Savior*. Once again, there are many Scriptures focused on us conforming our lives to His will.

Heavenly
Commander

Earthly
Companion

If we are not careful, pride can disrupt our growth. Jesus shared the following story, "The Pharisee stood by himself and prayed this prayer: 'I thank you, God, that I am not like other people—cheaters, sinners, adulterers. I'm certainly not like that tax collector! I fast twice a week, and I give you a tenth of my income'" (Luke 18:11-12). In the story, the Pharisee mistakenly attributed his ability to conform as righteousness. The Pharisee boasted about the very thing God hates. "God resists the proud" (1 Peter 5:5 NKJV).

Despite our best efforts, conformity is not sustainable. Adjustments are often short-term in nature. Although we actively take steps to conform to the image of God, there is an active current that resists our every effort. Even when we are successful, we are at risk. For instance, let's say I'm focusing on living a more holy lifestyle. My successful attempts to imitate Christ can lead me from living an unholy to a religious lifestyle. But my success may become overly legalistic, and I may go from holy to "holier than thou." My conditional success erodes my character into the very thing God finds vile, a prideful heart. As we fail, our eyes open to our need for something else, a more inclusive relationship. One not based solely on rules and directives. We begin to recognize the limits of conformity. Consider Paul's word after describing his failures, "Oh, what a miserable person I am! Who will free me from this life that is dominated by sin and death? Thank God! The answer is in Jesus Christ our Lord. So you see how it is: In my mind I really want to obey God's law, but because of my sinful nature I am a slave to sin"

(Rom. 7:24-25). Our frequent missteps actually lead us into greater dependence on God, as pride and condemnation give way to a humble heart.

Frustrated by our repeated failures, we cry out to our Lord with questions, and He meets us with dialogue. In many cases, we begin to negotiate between remorse and condemnation. Bringing our shortcomings and our failures to the Lord, we find repentance. He introduces us to His mercy, as our sins often go unpunished presently, even though we are deserving of judgment. In other cases, we stumble in condemnation as we fail to bring our failures to Him but focus on our lack of conformity. In these efforts of failing and re-engaging, of falling and getting up, the door opens to our deliverance. "The godly may trip seven times, but they will get up again" (Prov. 24:16). Trapped in our authoritative understanding of maturity, we define our growth by our ability to follow the rules and keep directives. Take a moment to contemplate the following question, "Where have you experienced failure in your pursuit of Christlikeness?"

# COGNITIVE CHRISTIANITY

Exclusive use of the Adjustment Response can leave us unbalanced. Conformity is not always positive. In the Old Testament, the children of Israel became interested in looking like other nations. In Samuel, we find the cautionary account. "'When that day comes, you will beg for relief from this king you are demanding, but then the Lord will not help you.' But the people refused to listen to Samuel's warning. 'Even so, we still want a king,' they said. 'We want to be like the nations around us. Our king will judge us and lead us into battle'" (1 Sam. 8:18-20). They rejected God's system of prophets to, instead, resemble their neighbors and enemies, succumbing to the cultural norms of having a king. In the New Testament, as Paul warned the Romans, "Don't copy the behavior and customs of this world" (Rom. 12:2). However, the error in both cases isn't *conforming*; it's what we are *conforming to*. In the first example, the nation of Israel was seeking to resemble its neighbors. In the second, Paul was warning the church in Rome not to resemble the world. Purely having an Adjustment Response makes us vulnerable to cultural kowtowing, which is to "show obsequious deference."[x]

Cognitive means "based on or capable of being reduced to empirical factual knowledge." We reduce our Christianity to operating within our capabilities or our "empirical factual knowledge."[xi] At times, our adjusting to His image may suffer due to our attraction to cultural norms. We have our own rules, laws, and traditions to which we hold ourselves and others accountable. The books we read, the clothes we wear, the music we listen to, the movies we watch, the food we eat and drink, etc. Like the Israelites, we are subject to the errors of culturally kowtowing.

Consider the Reverend Richard Furman, a contributing founder of Furman University. His life pursuits overlapped between spreading the gospel to save souls AND making the biblical case in defense of slavery in the South. Or, as recently as 2000[xii], one of the nation's finest Bible colleges did not accept interracial dating. Like slavery, this rule was primarily held in the South, as Southern Christians kowtowed to established Southern cultural norms. God's acting on behalf of the enslaved and examples of interracial marriage are both in the Bible. Let's not forget Moses' sister getting leprosy because she was upset with Moses' choice of an interracial spouse (Numbers 12). These believers erred as they stooped to the culture. Like cognitive scientists, their behavior was directed by their human perceptions and thoughts.

Even when we focus on aligning our life to biblical standards, we can lose sight of God. We can become intoxicated with customs and traditions. Consider Jesus' interactions with the religious elite. The Pharisees and Sadducees frequently confronted Jesus regarding following the law. On one occasion, the Pharisees and the disciples of John the Baptist were fasting, but Jesus' disciples were not. The Pharisees asked Jesus, "Why don't your disciples fast like John's disciples and the Pharisees do?" (Mark 2:18). Another time, Jesus' disciples were breaking off heads of grain to eat on the Sabbath. The Pharisees questioned His disciples' behavior saying, "Look, why are they breaking the law by harvesting grain on the Sabbath?" (Mark 2:24). I suppose the Pharisees obsessed over eating habits because, in a third instance, they inquired about the disciples' pre-meal rituals. Mark records that the Pharisees "noticed that some of his disciples failed to follow the Jewish ritual of hand washing before eating. (The Jews, especially the Pharisees, do not eat until they have poured water over their cupped hands, as required by their ancient traditions. Similarly, they don't eat anything from the market until they immerse their hands in water)" (Mark 7:2-4). After the third accusation regarding table etiquette, Jesus chastised the Pharisees by saying, "'These people honor me with their lips, / but their hearts are far from me. / Their worship is a farce, / for they teach man-made ideas as commands from God'" (Mark 7:6-7).

When we are conforming, it may look as though our hearts are in the right place, but we could be in error. The excessive pursuit of heavenly outcomes through rule-based living may result in legalism. Legalism is "the act of putting law above gospel by establishing requirements for salvation beyond repentance and faith in Jesus Christ and reducing the broad, inclusive and general precepts of the Bible to narrow and rigid moral codes."[xiii] We are also at risk of error as we conform based on our efforts and understanding of the Scriptures. The Pharisees questioned Jesus because the disciples were working on the Sabbath. Moses shared with Israel, "These are the instructions the Lord has commanded you to follow. You have six days each week for your ordinary work, but the seventh day must be a Sabbath day of complete rest, a holy day dedicated to the Lord. Anyone who works on that day must be put to death" (Ex. 35:1-2).

The Pharisees were not making outlandish legal claims. Still, Jesus chastised them because, despite their outward appearance regarding the laws, their hearts were not with Him. This focus on rules, ordinances, and legalism was often a stumbling block for the Pharisees and Sadducees and, in large parts, contributed to their crucifixion of Jesus. They effectively suffered from cognitive dissonance, as they stumbled over the inconsistencies between their expectations of Jesus and the actions and attitudes He exhibited. In many cases, we are leading our efforts to conform, and we can get it wrong. Left to ourselves, like the Pharisees and Saul, we can persecute the very people our Creator loves.

## *What Would Jesus Do?*

Even today, we perpetuate a cognitive Christianity approach to our faith as we wrestle with questions like What Would Jesus Do (WWJD)? Imagine if I was contemplating a parental decision. "What would my grandfather do?" I'd revisit his letters and spend time remembering his actions and words. I would take this approach because my grandfather died several years ago; he is no longer available for me to ask him. Alternatively, I might ask my dad because he's alive. And he may remind me of things my grandfather wrote, did, and said. He will help me to navigate the decision.

Jesus is alive, but too often, we interact with Him as though He's dead. What Would Jesus Do thinking is our rational understanding of Jesus' thoughts. In this example, it is my approach to my grandfather's advice. Instead of asking Jesus, we take action based on our *understanding* of His actions. A cognitive, dead approach is a poor substitution for a relationship with a living God. Consider the following warning, "Trust in the Lord with all your heart; / do not depend on your own understanding. / Seek his will in all you do, / **and he will show you which path to take**" (Prov. 3:5-6, emphasis mine). God's role is active. But too often, we do the exact opposite. Although well-meaning, our What Would Jesus Do approach is distorted and more reflective of What Jesus Wouldn't Do. Our WWJD approach entices us to lean on our understanding. And we fail to seek and trust Him and allow Him to direct our paths. This course of action falls short of the divine relationship He's invited us to.

## ELLIE THE POSSUM

A light-hearted illustration of ill-suited conformity is the actress Queen Latifah and her role as Ellie in the movie *Ice Age*. Ellie is a female mammoth who became separated from her herd as a calf. After being grafted into a loving family of possums, she grew up believing that she was indeed a possum. It's hilarious. She hangs from trees, plays dead, and lives off worms and snails. Ellie grows into a ten-foot, six-ton mammoth who *believes* she is a possum. The situation is comical until circumstances call for her strength as a mammoth, and Ellie continues to function as a possum. Many of us are mammoths posing as possums.

This ill-suited conformity comes at a high price. My thoughts immediately go to my beloved grandfather. Pop-pop served as an infantryman in War World II. He was a protector, a defender. He was the kind of guy you wanted on the perimeter, daring the world to break through. Not surprisingly, he was so proud of me when I was accepted into West Point. The oath I took as a cadet was seemingly written off the pages of his heart: "support and defend the Constitution of the United States against all enemies, foreign or domestic."[xiv]

My grandfather was the second African American police officer in Trenton, N.J. He loved *being* a police officer. He was created to be a protector. But one day, his church leadership admonished him to let go of law enforcement because they deemed it *inappropriate.* It didn't *conform* to their image of God; I still wonder if they were familiar with Abraham, Joshua, David, Samson, the Old Testament, etc. My grandfather was encouraged to get a job that didn't interfere with his "ecclesiastical duties," and, sadly, he did. I believe this decision broke his heart. I remember seeing my grandfather coming home from his new job with the state, joyless, empty, alive, but not fully living. Created a mammoth, yet living as a possum. Like Saul on the road to Damascus, we need something higher than conformity, and as we mature from Heavenly Commander to the next blend, a shift occurs.

# RECAP

- The Adjustment Response consists of mission-focused behavior with celestial objectives.

- It shares the characteristic of conditional statements, but the if-then statements assume a spiritual bend (i.e., Beatitudes).

- The Adjustment Response helps us to conform to godly directives.

- Practically, as we apply the Scriptures to our lives, we begin to resemble our Creator's divine nature.

- This blend encourages us to *imitate* Christ.

- An exclusive use of the Adjustment Response can leave us unbalanced. (i.e., the Israelites rejected God's system of prophets and conformed to the hierarchy of their neighbors and enemies.)

- In error, a Heavenly Commander blend may be subject to cultural kowtowing.

- Even when we focus on conforming our living biblically, we can also lose sight of God and become intoxicated with customs and traditions.

- The excessive pursuit of heavenly outcomes through rule-based living may result in legalism.

- Key biblical stories: Jailer (Acts 16), Israelites wanting a king (1 Samuel 8), and the Pharisees (Mark 2 and 7)

**CHAPTER 3**

# A SHIFT: GROWING BEYOND COMMANDS AND CONFORMITY

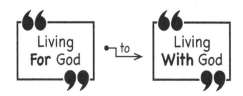

## GARDEN FLAVORED

"It was the law that showed me my sin. I would never have known that coveting is wrong if the law had not said, 'You must not covet.'" (Rom. 7:7)

The existence of law and order is not always stifling. There is sensemaking to coloring within the lines. Many view obedience as an outdated orthodoxy, purposed to limit our freedom of expression. In our plight for freedom and autonomy, we often view boundaries as a means to prevent our enjoyment. But God's directives are not aimed at preventing enjoyment, but rather to usher us into more enduring and fulfilling experiences. This was evident from the very beginning, as humanity lived with God naked and unafraid.

Before Eve's inception, God directs Adam, "You may freely eat the fruit of every tree in the garden—except the tree of the knowledge of good and evil. If you eat its fruit, you are sure to die" (Genesis 2:16-17). And for the first time, God introduces man to a delectable fruit not meant to be consumed. Shortly following this dietary restriction, God diagnoses Adam's need—"It is not good for the man to be alone. I will make a helper who is just right for him" (Gen. 2:18). Then God parades before Adam living creatures made by His hand. Wild animals, birds, and livestock, all marvelous, but none fit to be Adam's companion. Then, from the one He had created, He creates. And God fashions a perfect fit, which completes humanity and leaves Adam mesmerized.

I don't know how long Adam and Eve spent in the garden before being evicted; I just wish it had been longer. Seemingly within a breath of being naked and unashamed, the honeymoon couple stumbled across the threshold of sin. I pause at that initial thought: Naked, before God, and unashamed. No secrets. No coverings. No excuses. Humankind, standing as is, before the Great I AM, without hesitation or trepidation. And at that moment, feeling no disgrace or fear, like an infant child in the presence of his loving father. Humanity walks around completely naked, leaving modesty to the wind. Adam and Eve are exposed, vulnerable, and uncovered.

All is well, until an encounter with God's most cunning creation. Beginning with a seemingly harmless inquiry, the serpent asks Eve, "Did God really say you must not eat the fruit from any of the trees in the garden?" (Gen. 3:1). The serpent misstates God's command. Eve corrects the seemingly purposeful error. She clarifies the command; "It's only the fruit from the tree in the middle of the garden that we are not allowed to eat. God said, 'You must not eat it or even touch it; if you do, you will die'" (Gen. 3:3).

The serpent's guile grows more direct, "You won't die!" (Gen. 3:4), as he brashly contradicts the consequence of disobeying God. The cunning serpent saves his deadliest suggestion for last. "God knows that your eyes will be opened as soon as you eat it, and you will be like God, knowing both good and evil" (Gen 3:5). His last lie seeds God's command as a boundary to prevent Eve's growth and enjoyment. And so, Eve and Adam consume the serpent's distorted view of God, and devouring the fruit quickly follows. They eat because they accept a picture of God's Commanding nature as restrictive and hindering.

And what followed their consumption of the luscious fruit? Did they become "like God"? No, they found themselves naked, crafting poorly fitted clothes out of leaves, hiding in the woods. They found themselves with a new emotion…fear—what a juxtaposition. Humanity beginning in an unfettered relationship with a creator God, vulnerable yet fearless. Yet, through our freedom of expression, we found ourselves more knowledgeable yet fearful. No longer free, we became bound to a sinful nature.

God introduced resistance to develop our character, not erode it. Restraint is not intended to push us further from God but to knit our hearts closer to His. Physically, countertraction exercises build muscle, strengthen our core, and increase our endurance. The prodigal son's delayed inheritance was not designed to keep him from his riches but to build, strengthen, and prepare him for them. Spiritually, restraint serves to demonstrate our trust in God and facilitates the building of our faith. In the garden, God introduced choice, providing mankind with the opportunity to demonstrate our trust in Him.

Today, like the inaugural couple, we leave order behind in pursuit of freedom. We exchange the promises of God for the allure of strange fruit, and we awake to our own nakedness and fear. These false promises prompted Adam and Eve's misconstrued attempts for knowledge, Samson's thirst for Delilah, Israel's desire for a king, Judas' distorted wish for a more plausible savior, and our longings for all manner of perverted produce. We resemble the prodigal son, making choices according to our own pubescent will. God has always pursued us. Yet, we resist His order and elect alternatives because of our fears, inhibitions, doubts, and desires.

Having a distorted view of God is restrictive and debilitating. We must pursue God's nature in wholeness and balance.

# A FAILED SHIFT

An exclusive focus on God's Commander nature can leave us distorted. This point is evident in the biblical account of the rich, young ruler. As previously mentioned, he was a boss, but he recognized that something was missing from his life. He pursues Jesus and asks, "What must I do to live forever?" Jesus responds with conditionality, a list of dos and don'ts. The young man responds with conditional performance, "I've done all of these things since I was a kid." In a world constructed on if…then statements, he is performing well. His obedience seemingly contributed to his success as he is rich and ruling at a young age. But even though he was proficient at law and order, he was hungry for something more. As an outward act of submission, he kneels at Jesus' feet. Then Jesus says, "If you want to be perfect, go and sell all your possessions and give the money to the poor, and you will have treasure in heaven. **Then come, follow me**" (Matt. 19:21, emphasis mine). The rich, young ruler recognizes the inadequacy of simply pursuing God's Commanding nature. The rules are not enough. He had successfully interacted with the Lord's authoritative nature since he was a kid; nonetheless, he finds himself wanting. Jesus' response was an invitation for him to go beyond living *for* God and begin living *with* Him…"Come, follow me." Unfortunately, the rich young ruler was more comfortable following commandments then following Jesus. He wasn't the only one.

At eight years old, Josiah became the king of Israel. He was a descendant of wicked kings. His grandfather, Manasseh, led Israel into more debauchery than Israel's enemies (2 Chr. 33:9). And his father, Amon, also forsook God. These failures provoked God to promise Jerusalem's destruction. But unlike his forefathers, King Josiah walked in obedience. He authored the repair of God's temple. In his eighteenth year, the nation is in the middle of refurbishing the tabernacle. Josiah sends Shaphan, his scribe, to the high priest overseeing the work with money to cover labor and materials.

In the process of repairing the temple, Hilkiah, the high priest, discovers The Book of the Law. The title reinforces the idea that God values law. Josiah orders Shaphan to read the book in his presence. When Josiah hears The Book of the Law, he is devastated. He tears his clothes in grief as he recognizes that Israel is actively sinning against God. The young king humbles himself and leads his nation into repentance. He tears down idols, destroys the altars of false gods, and removes wicked priests. Celebrating the Passover like never before, he directs Israel back toward God (2 Kings 23:25). Notwithstanding King Josiah's faithfulness, God is still intent on destroying Jerusalem.

God selects the Egyptian king Neco as His weapon of judgment against Israel. King in the tradition of kings, Josiah defends against the Egyptians' assault. King Neco sends messengers to King Josiah, saying, "What do you want with me, king of Judah? I have no quarrel with you today! I am on my way to fight another nation, and God has told me to hurry! Do not interfere with God, who is with me, or he will destroy you" (2 Chron. 35:21). In this paradoxical moment, King Josiah's enemy is in alignment with God's intent, the destruction of Jerusalem. Neco warns Josiah to concede, but the young king will not yield. While Neco is fighting *with* God, Josiah dies on the battlefield fighting *for* God's people.

We, like biblical characters, can find ourselves amid a failed shift. We opt to continue in living for God, when He is calling us into something deeper. Outwardly, living for God appears centered on God's will. But underneath, it may be anchored to our own nature. Living for God shines bright and rings with promise. It resounds with, "For the King of Kings and Lord of Lords!" It echoes a heartfelt cry, declaring our allegiances as we prepare to take action. But in the absence of God's complete nature, it's *almost* true. In living for God, we prioritize logic and conditionality. We grow comfortable with Christianity as a religion, but we miss the intent of a *personal* relationship with God. Our devotion faintly grows beyond adherence, as our desires rest upon making it to heaven. Good things, but as we've seen in the accounts of the crowd of 5,000, Josiah, and others, good things can stand in the way of God. Pursuing God solely based upon His Commanding nature may lead to the following drawbacks: (1) stumbling at God's incongruent nature, (2) focusing on commands more than the Commander, or (3) accepting a distant and disconnected relationship with God.

# INCONGRUENCE

Incongruence is defined as "not the same, not compatible or out of place."[xv] At times, God's nature stands at odds with rational expectations, and His decisions seem out of place. Consider the following two verses. "Don't answer the foolish arguments of fools, or you will become as foolish as they are" (Prov. 26:4). The following verse reads, "Be sure to answer the foolish arguments of fools, or they will become wise in their own estimation" (Prov. 26:5). How do we fulfill them both? This biblical conundrum frustrates some, while many awkwardly avoid the incongruence. The answer doesn't rest in reasoning.

> "My thoughts are nothing like your thoughts," says the Lord.
> "And my ways are far beyond anything you could imagine.
> For just as the heavens are higher than the earth,
> so my ways are higher than your ways
> and my thoughts higher than your thoughts." (Isaiah 55:8-9)

Incongruence is part of His nature.

Living only through God's Commander nature overvalues our mental abilities and undervalues God's incongruence. God's thoughts often conflict with our own. The Lord promised Abram, *the Father of Faith*, a son (Gen. 15:4). Rationally, Abram and Sarai are old, and not getting any younger. Sarai is not getting pregnant. In an attempt to fulfill God's promise, Sarai suggests Abram father a child through her handmaiden, Hagar. Ishmael is born, but God's promise remains unfulfilled. The Lord's approach conflicts with Abram's understanding. It is incongruent. God invites us to walk with Him amid these conflicting facts. "Trust in the Lord with all your heart, / And lean not on your own understanding; / In all your ways acknowledge Him, / And He shall direct your paths" (Prov. 3:5-6 NKJV).

Those that walked with Jesus struggled with His incongruence. The miraculously fed crowd "began to murmur in disagreement because he had said, 'I am the bread that came down from heaven.' They said, 'Isn't this Jesus, the son of Joseph? We know his father and mother. How can he say, "I came down from heaven"?'" (John 6:41-42). Jesus' words conflicted with their understanding, incongruence ensued, and they stumbled.

Jesus' disciples struggled as well. John explained, "Jesus was aware that his disciples were complaining, so he said to them, 'Does this offend you?'" (John 6:61). The Scripture continues, "At this point many of his disciples turned away and deserted him" (John 6:66). As an interesting aside, a verse describing people deserting Jesus is 6:66. The reality of Jesus was inconsistent with their expectation of Jesus, and the incongruence led to offense and broken relationship.

In the military, we used the term "LIMFAC" to describe the limiting factor in an operation. For instance, the LIMFAC in moving troops from one location to another may be the number of trucks that are available. When our relationship with God is based only on His Commanding nature, the LIMFAC is logic and performance. In the 2016 movie *"Superman vs. Batman,"* the villain Lex Luthor postulates, "If God is all-powerful, He cannot be good; if God is good, He cannot be all-powerful!"[xvi] Like those before us, when God's actions don't meet our expectations, we trip over our logic.

During times of incongruence, a lesser exchange becomes tempting. We consider a trade for something more manageable and less majestic. We look for conditions that are more understandable and prefer reason over the depth of mystery. Like the deepest corners of space or the unexplored sea canyons, mystery pushes us beyond the depths of our understanding. The enigmatic takes us beyond our reach and compels us to opt for things more sensible. The Israelites erected a calf out of silver and gold to explain their deliverance. We construct theories that are more explainable and controllable than God's incongruent nature. In the face of the unexplainable, we accept logic, which later proves to be illogical. We prefer a flat earth to the phenomenon of a planet rotating on its axis while traveling around the sun. As toddlers, we stand with a clutched fist and infantile resolve as we reach out to pet a tiger while uttering "kitty-cat."

When questioned regarding His incongruent nature, God responded to Job saying, "Do you still want to argue with the Almighty? / You are God's critic, but do you have the answers?" (Job 40:2). Nicodemus showed us a better way in John 3. He opted for mystery over understanding when Jesus explained the need for us to be "born again." Although God's Commander nature is scripturally supported and productive, there is evidence of a part of His nature that is less logical and ordered.

# FOCUS

The second drawback to concentrating purely on God's Commanding nature is pursuing commands to the exclusion of knowing the Commander. It's easy for us to become paralyzed by our needs. At times, in the pursuit of provision, we lose sight of the Provider. Nine of the ten leapers healed by Jesus failed to say thank you (Luke 17). They became engrossed in their healing but never became engrossed in Jesus. So often, we are no different. With eyes fixed on our needs and desires, we emphasize Jesus' fruitfulness but not our relationship with Him. As a result, many of our actions reflect nothing more than conditional attempts to "eat of the loaves and be filled."

The apostle Peter hesitated when told, "Get up, Peter; kill and eat them" (Acts 10:13). As he looked across a picnic, filled with four-footed animals, Peter responded, "No, Lord...I have never eaten anything that our Jewish laws have declared impure and unclean" (Acts 10:14). He was more concerned with adhering to the Levitical laws of nutritional obedience than *actually* responding to the voice of the Lord. The rich young ruler was interested in earning eternal life but became disinterested in life with Jesus. We frequently focus on following rules instead of following Jesus. The Lord's visit to the home of two sisters illustrates this point.

Martha and Mary invited Jesus and His disciples into their home. Martha busies herself, preparing for their guests. Martha, surrounded by hungry guests, observes her sister Mary isn't helping. Mary is less interested in being a good hostess and gives her attention to Jesus' teachings as she sits at the Lord's feet. Martha rebels. In a you've-got-to-be-kidding-me moment, Martha turns to the guest of honor and says, "Lord, doesn't it seem unfair to you that my sister just sits here while I do all the work? Tell her to come and help me" (Luke 10:40). Martha's request seems reasonable. There is work to do and people to serve. Mary is sitting while Martha is serving. Yet Jesus' words are clear, "Martha, Martha, you are worried and troubled about many things. But one thing is needed, and Mary has chosen that good part, which will not be taken away from her" (Luke 10:41-42 NKJV).

Many of us are focused on the duties and responsibilities of Christianity. We lead lives consistent with Scripture and Christian traditions. Cloaked in servanthood, our competing demands appear to be God-honoring. Like Martha, we are careful about directives, commands, traditions, etc., but only "one thing is needful." Have we chosen to ignore good things to spend time at Jesus' feet, or are we just content with being busy?

# DISTANT AND DISCONNECTED

An unbalanced Commander view can also lead us away from the Lord. In commands and conditionality, we fail to view ourselves as God's children and friends, and we resolve only to see ourselves as His servants and soldiers. In these distortions, God remains a distant king, and we embrace His precepts while rejecting His grace. Consequently, we accept interacting with the Lord primarily through our pastor, congregational services, and group activities. In fanatical duty and law, requests for provisions and repentance dominate our prayers without the tenderness of dialogue. Sadly, our interactions with the Lord are less personal and seldom resemble the fondness between a bride and her groom.

Jesus, speaking to the disciples, shared, "When you pray, don't babble on and on as the Gentiles do. They think their prayers are answered merely by repeating their words again and again. Don't be like them, for your Father knows exactly what you need even before you ask him!" (Matt. 6:7-8). Our prayers aren't meant to be lifeless, structured repeats. When teaching His disciples how to pray, Jesus said, "Pray **like** this." It's an example of how to begin a dialogue, not a recitation. Our prayers were never intended to be a monologue. Through conversation, we learn more about our Creator and more about ourselves.

But our exchanges with the Lord often parallel the Old Testament Israelites who implored Moses to speak with God on their behalf. They withdrew from God instead of drawing closer. Inside the Jerusalem temple, there was a curtain that separated the place of worship from the Holy of Holies (Hebrews 9:3). The place was so reverential that the high priest only entered once a year. Even then, the priest's entrance was proceeded by blood sacrifices for his sins and the sins of the people (Heb. 9:7). But after Jesus' death, the veil, which was intended to separate us from God, was torn from top to bottom (Matt. 27:51) to restore our relationship *with* the Original Author.

Nonetheless, many of us remain in the metaphorical outer courts. We stand beyond the place where the veil once draped when God has invited us to enter in. Keeping our distance, we peer inside, intrigued and curious. But instead of stepping forward, we maintain a relationship with the Lord through the lives of others or through rules and traditions. With needle and thread, we approximate the edges of the torn veil in a misguided attempt to reconstruct the torn separation, which leads to misrepresenting intimacy through proxy. As a result, we grow to view God as distant and disconnected.

It's easy to become disoriented and distant from the truth of God's nature. In his article "The Art of Failure," Malcolm Gladwell discusses John F. Kennedy, Jr.'s fatal crash. While flying on a hazy night, Kennedy became disoriented. The plane entered into a spiral dive and eventually crashed. Before the crash, Kennedy attempted to re-orient himself by changing direction, speed, and altitude, without success. Gladwell shared that, "In a spiral dive, though, the effect of the plane's G-force on the inner ear means that the pilot *feels* perfectly level even if the plane is not."[xvii] Many of us *feel* as though our relationship with God, characterized by church attendance and Bible reading, is balanced. But do we know Him, do we listen to His voice, are we following Him, or are we unknowingly in a spiral dive? (See John 10:27.)

Beyond God's Commanding nature is an invitation for us to come closer. Not replacing His authority but building upon it. The author of Hebrews penned, "This High Priest of ours understands our weaknesses, for he faced all of the same testings we do, yet he did not sin. So let us come boldly to the throne of our gracious God. There we will receive his mercy, and we will find grace to help us when we need it most" (Heb. 4:15-16). Our earthly needs touch our Lord, and we are invited to come before Him boldly. In perversion, we mistake focusing on God meeting our needs and focusing our attention on conforming to His Word as a life exemplative of remaining in Him. But now is the occasion where we must walk through the veil and allow ourselves to abide. Now is the time to shift beyond...

# FROM COMMANDER TO COMPANION

The Awareness and Adjustment Responses portrayed in the earlier blends yield productivity and conformity, respectively. And both of these blends are important, but neither represents a complete picture of God's nature. The Commander authoritative orientations dominate our view of God, especially for men. Consequently, we settle for conformity, at best, in place of unity. Conforming involves adjusting our behavior to resemble the standard or desired performance. Conversely, unity is "the state of being united or joined as a whole."[xviii] Paul said that as we grow in Christ, we should be continually conforming to His image (Rom. 8:29).

But Jesus prayed for something more. Jesus prayed that we would be one, even as He and His Father are one. He described this further, "I pray that they will all be one, just as you and I are one—as you are in me, Father, and I am in you" (John 17:21). He prayed that we would be fully integrated with and encompassed by Him. The appearance of conformity on the outside may be disingenuous on the inside (i.e., Judas). Alternatively, what appears to be un-conformed on the outside may be united on the inside. Jesus explained,

"But what do you think about this? A man with two sons told the older boy, 'Son, go out and work in the vineyard today.' The son answered, 'No, I won't go,' but later he changed his mind and went anyway" (Matt. 21:28-29). Behavior agreed to (or refused) sometimes differs from behavior performed.

At times, we encourage people to conform to what we deem to be acceptable. We come across men, like John the Baptist, clothed with camel's hair and leather, living on a diet of locust and honey (Matt. 3:4), not fitting into our standards or norms. Or we encounter someone leaping and dancing before the Lord and, like Michal (David's wife), try to tone them down (2 Sam. 6:16, 20). Or, like the Pharisees, we pedestal religious behavior, such as fasting or traditional Sabbath protocol. And inadvertently, we find ourselves encouraging conformity at the expense of an individual's unity with God. Conformity unchecked would have every member of the body acting like a single member. But as Paul shared, "The human body has many parts, but the many parts make up one whole body. So it is with the body of Christ" (1 Cor. 12:12). Jesus never prioritized conformity over unity. We must be cautious not to either. God's Commanding nature focuses on our physical ailments, financial needs, maintaining our salvation, and demonstrating our Christlikeness. There is a transition from God's Commanding nature to His Companion nature, where we mature from simply living *for* God to living *with* Him.

# RECAP

- God introduced resistance to develop our character, not erode it.

- Like Adam and Eve, we leave order behind in pursuit of freedom and exchange God's promises for the allure of strange fruit, and we awake to our own nakedness and fear.

- We must pursue God's nature in wholeness and balance. An exclusive focus on God's Commander nature can leave us distorted.

- We, like biblical characters, can find ourselves amid a failed shift. We opt to continue in living for God, when He is calling us into something deeper.

- Pursuing God solely based upon His Commanding nature may lead to the following drawbacks: (1) stumbling at God's incongruent nature, (2) focusing on commands more than the Commander, or (3) accepting a distant and disconnected relationship with God.

- During times of incongruence, we look for conditions that are more understandable and prefer reason over the depth of mystery.

- Many of us are focused on the duties and responsibilities of Christianity. Like Martha, we are careful about directives, commands, traditions, etc., but only "one thing is needful."

- In commands and conditionality, we fail to view ourselves as God's children and friends, and we resolve only to see ourselves as His servants and soldiers.

- There is a transition from God's Commanding nature to His Companion nature, where we mature from simply living for God to living with Him.

- Key biblical stories: Adam and Eve (Gen. 2 and 3), rich young ruler (Matt. 19), King Josiah (2 Kings 23, 2 Chron. 35), and Martha and Mary (Luke 10)

# CHAPTER 4

# THIRD BLEND: EARTHLY COMPANION

## DAMASCUS ROAD

In the midst of a riotous mob stands a man boldly directing his comments toward the Jewish high council. Because of poor rationing and the ill-treatment of widows, the disciples had selected Stephen and others to serve. But Stephen's contributions would go well beyond meal allocations. Amid false accusations, he confidently recounts key moments of Jewish history. He begins with God appearing to Abraham in Mesopotamia and concludes with the Messiah's betrayal and murder. His words pierce the ears of the Pharisees, while his face illuminates. With each word, the Jewish leaders grow increasingly incensed, contriving how they might shut him up for good. Stephen gazes into heaven. Jesus stands up. And Stephen shares what he sees, "Look, I see the heavens opened and the Son of Man standing in the place of honor at God's right hand!" (Acts 7:56). The mob can't take another utterance. They grab Stephen, drag him outside of the city walls, and hurl stones at God's defenseless servant. A young man gleefully watches over the coats of Stephen's assailants, allowing the accusers to assault God's servant unencumbered. And on a day when the ground ran red with Stephen's blood, Saul, a Pharisee of Pharisees, was fashioned.

Saul was not your ordinary Pharisee. In a letter to the Philippians, he shared glimpses of his childhood, "I was circumcised when I was eight days old" (Phil. 3:5). He further described himself, saying, "I am a pure-blooded citizen of Israel and a member of the tribe of Benjamin—a real Hebrew if there ever was one! I was a member of the Pharisees, who demand the strictest obedience to the Jewish law. I was so zealous that I harshly persecuted the church. And as for righteousness, I obeyed the law without fault" (Phil. 3:5-6). What a juxtaposition. Saul was a member of the group with the strictest obedience to Jewish law, a group which was committed to destroying the church. Saul was relentless. His thoughts revolved around persecuting the church, and Jerusalem wasn't enough. He sought to extend his oppressive campaign 200 miles northward into Damascus (Acts 9). Saul petitioned the high priest for permission to raid the Damascus synagogues in search of "followers of the Way." He intended to find Jesus' followers hiding in this distant city and bring them back to Jerusalem in chains. The high priest, pleased with Saul's ambition, authorized the expedition. But Saul was interrupted along the way.

As Saul journeys to Damascus, he sees a light so intense that it causes him to drop to the ground. A voice follows, "Saul! Saul! Why are you persecuting me?" (Acts 9:4). Saul doesn't know whom he is talking to, but he recognizes authority. He responds, "Who are you, Lord?" (Acts 9:5 NKJV). And the voice from heaven replies, "I am Jesus, whom you are persecuting" (Acts 9:5 NKJV). Both fearful and bewildered, Saul awakens to a God he never knew. He responds to the voice, saying, "Lord, what do You want me to do?" (Acts 9:6 NKJV). And the Lord answers, "Arise and go into the city, and you will be told what you must do" (Acts 9:6 NKJV). Saul gets up from the ground, blinded. The men that accompanied him stand speechless, seeing nothing but hearing everything. And Saul enters Damascus, no longer full of hubris, but humility.

# EARTHLY COMPANION NATURE EXPLAINED

In God's Earthly Companion nature, we discover God walking with us in our earthly circumstances. In this blend, God does not interact with us only through law and order, but through His unconditional love. We experience grace, independent of conditional performance. As a murderer, Saul's actions were punishable by either death or exile. But God, in His Earthly Companion nature, unconditionally extended His grace. Departing from human reasoning, this blend is much like the proverbial bumblebee. It's an insect with short wings and a fat body type that should prevent it from flying, yet it flies. Within the Companion blend, we are taken aback by the godly incongruence.

We see this as Ananias and others are startled by Saul's role in God's plan. Saul resembled a pharisaical Sicario, a modern-day hitman, who was known for dragging men and women from their homes, imprisoning some and killing others (Acts 8:3). It's no surprise that the faithful hesitated at Saul's newfound faith. When God directed Ananias to go and meet with Saul, he replied,

> "But Lord… I've heard many people talk about the terrible things this man has done to the believers in Jerusalem! And he is authorized by the leading priests to arrest everyone who calls upon your name." But the Lord said, "Go, for Saul is my chosen instrument

to take my message to the Gentiles and to kings, as well as to the people of Israel." (Acts 9:13-15)

God exhibited His incongruent nature.

In this blend, God chooses not only to be known as King but as Savior, Bridegroom, Comforter, and Friend. These names are suggestively inclusive. God with us. Scripture exhaustively exemplifies this connectedness. Enoch and Noah walked with God (Gen. 5:24, Gen. 6:9). Abram talked with God (Gen. 17:3). Israel had power with God (Gen. 32:28). Moses delivered Israel with God (Ex. 3:12). Joshua took over for Moses with God (Joshua 1:9). David pleaded with God (2 Sam. 12:16). Jesus was named Emmanuel, which literally means "God with us" (Matt. 1:23). As we walk with the Lord and communicate with Him, the distance between us decreases. The author of James encouraged this bonding, saying, "Come close to God, and God will come close to you" (James 4:8).

In this aspect of His nature, God interacts with us in unique personal experiences. Through heuristics, we deepen our relationship with God. The definition of heuristics is "enabling a person to discover or learn something for themselves."[xix] Through God's Companion nature, we discover God in ways that are specific to us. In Saul's experience, he began as a self-confessed legal zealot. Remember his self-characterization: circumcised at eight days old, a pure-blooded Benjamite (a real Hebrew), a Pharisee of the strictest order (Phil. 3:5). Translation from Greek to our vernacular: Saul was a religious O.G., a boss of bosses. He was the embodiment of ecclesiastical fire. No one was more judicious in his approach to God than him. But his pursuit of God, through law and conformity, resulted in persecuting Jesus. Saul's attempts to live for God led him to imprison, torture, and kill Jesus' followers. Saul had the law, but he hadn't had a personal experience with Jesus. Heuristically speaking, he hadn't discovered God for himself until that Damascus road.

Within this blend, God joins us in our messy circumstances, sometimes related to health, finances, or our general welfare. God's Companion nature accompanies us. And through His presence, we "experience God's peace, which exceeds anything we can understand" (Phil. 4:7). Because of this companionship, Stephen chose dialogue with Christ in the midst of martyrdom. He spoke to Jesus, saying, "Lord Jesus, receive my spirit" (Acts 7:59) and "Lord, don't charge them with this sin!" (Acts 7:60). Stephen didn't focus on escape. And without request, Jesus granted him sleep while being stoned.

The Earthly Companion blend is known as the **Abandonment** Response. Within it, we discover God's Earthly Companion nature as we abandon all else for Him. Abandon means "to give up to the control or influence of another person," or "to give up with the intent of never again claiming a right or interest in."[xx] The rich young ruler was not willing to give up control. He was not willing to give up his riches with the intent of never again claiming a right to them. He was willing to adjust his life based on rules and commands, but he was not willing to abandon his riches. Contrastingly, Peter said to Jesus, "We've given up everything to follow you. What will we get?" (Matt. 19:27). The answer, Jesus' presence. "Jesus replied, 'I assure you that when the world is made new and the Son of Man sits upon his glorious throne, you who have been my followers will also sit on twelve thrones, judging the twelve tribes of Israel'" (Matt. 19:28).

The apostle Luke illustrated what abandonment looks like to Jesus. The Scriptures recount,

> He said to another person, "Come, follow me."
> The man agreed, but he said, "Lord, first let me return home and bury my father."
> But Jesus told him, "Let the spiritually dead bury their own dead! Your duty is to go and preach about the Kingdom of God."
> Another said, "Yes, Lord, I will follow you, but first let me say good-bye to my family."
> But Jesus told him, "Anyone who puts a hand to the plow and then looks back is not fit for the Kingdom of God." (Luke 9:59-62)

When given the opportunity to follow Jesus, returning home to bury a loved one is not abandoning. Taking time to say good-bye to the family is not surrendering. Beginning to follow Jesus but looking back is not forsaking. The Abandonment Response to Jesus can be summarized in three simple words, "Come, follow me" (Luke 9:59). When we surrender all else to follow Jesus, we experience God for ourselves. My dad would say, "A man with an argument is always at the mercy of a man with an experience." The following table summarizes the Abandonment Response.

### 7 Characteristics of the Abandonment Response

| | |
|---:|---|
| Focus | Walking "with" God |
| Context | Unconditional approach |
| Roles | Bridegroom/bride, Father/child, Comforter/comforted |
| Communication | Dialogue with the Lord |
| Proximity | Closer; as we draw near to Him, He draws near to us |
| Choice | Free to make choices in earthly circumstances |
| Pleasing God | Abiding with Him despite present conditions |

# CHRYSALIS AND COFFIN

God's Earthly Companion nature differs from His Heavenly Commander nature. In the previous blend, we were working to conform, but within the Earthly Companion blend, God is driving the change. As we walk *with* the Creator, we **transform**. God's presence is transforming. Consider the account of a few guys who were burying a friend. As they buried him, they saw a group of Moabite raiders. They had to get out of there. "So they hastily threw the corpse into the tomb of Elisha and fled. But as soon as the body touched Elisha's bones, the dead man revived and jumped to his feet!" (2 Kings 13:21). They were not seeking healing for their beloved. He was already dead. They were not going before the priest, looking for a resurrection. They had accepted the fact that their friend had died. They were looking to lay his bones to rest. But when their friend's bones came in contact with a man who had spent so much time in God's presence, a transformation occurred.

A transformation is "thorough or dramatic change in the form, appearance, or character of."[xxi] A divine transformation consists of three critical elements: a dramatic change (in form, appearance, or character), a divine encounter (presence), and death (ashes). Let's explore the element of dramatic change. One of my favorite biblical accounts occurs in Paul's letter to the Romans. He shares, "For ever since the world was created, people have seen the earth and sky. Through everything God made, they can clearly see his invisible qualities—his eternal power and divine nature. So they have no excuse for not knowing God" (Rom. 1:20). God's earthly creations help us to understand His nature. As such, a caterpillar helps us to understand transformations. When a caterpillar transforms into a butterfly, its visible shape is entirely different—the appearance and character of the insect changes from grounded to flying. Conformity is a caterpillar imitating a butterfly, but transformation is a caterpillar becoming a butterfly.

The second element in transformation is divine presence. The apostle Paul wrote, "And do not be conformed to this world, but be transformed by the renewing of your mind, that you may prove what is that good and acceptable and perfect will of God" (Rom. 12:2 NKJV). The word "renew" means to make like new. When a car is renewed, it is restored to its manufactured conditions. If a table is renewed, it is restored to its original form. For us, transformation requires a renewing of the mind. The car and the table cannot regenerate themselves; they need the assistance of a mechanic or a carpenter. Too often, we operate under the assumption that we can renew our own minds. But we, like the table, need the help of the Carpenter.

Renewing requires assistance from someone who understands the manufacturer's original specifications. "And yet, O Lord, you are our Father. / We are the clay, and you are the potter. / We all are formed by your hand" (Isa. 64:8). These transformations are no more self-induced than Saul initiating his experience on the Damascus road. To be transformed, the Lord's presence is required. Jesus shared, "Remain in me, and I will remain in you. For a branch cannot produce fruit if it is severed from the vine, and you cannot be fruitful unless you remain in me" (John 15:4). Like the caterpillar is encapsulated in the chrysalis, or a moth in a cocoon, we must become surrounded and insulated in Christ.

The third element required is death or ashes. This transformative process, for the caterpillar and us, is contingent upon what we are *in*. For the caterpillar, it must remain *in* the chrysalis, while we must remain *in* Christ. The similarities are startling. Once inside the chrysalis, the caterpillar's old body dies, and a different creature forms within a new, protective shell. The transformation occurs from the inside out, as the caterpillar uses the digestive fluids that once broke food down to consume and break down its own body.[xxii] The chrysalis stage is the period of time the caterpillar is in the chrysalis. It can span from a period of a few days to a couple of weeks. Some species have emerged from their chrysalises after a few years due to extreme environmental conditions, like a drought.[xxiii]

The caterpillar's chrysalis can be likened to a human's coffin as Christ invites us to die to ourselves. The process is uniquely personal, with some of us emerging from abiding in our chrysalis for years because of extreme conditions. Our transformation occurs from the inside out as we die and are born again in His regenerative process. The apostle Paul shared, "It doesn't matter whether we have been circumcised or not. What counts is whether we have been transformed into a new creation" (Gal. 6:15). Conformity addresses the outward appearance, but it does not change the internal.

Through God's participative nature, change results in unprecedented newness in this present world.

This element captures the essence of the Abandonment Response. Ashes are the leftover remains of something that has died or has been destroyed. Our Creator instituted an exchange of "beauty for ashes" (Isa. 61:3). Worthless ashes exchanged for priceless beauty. This exchange is for ashes only. Cleaning up before seeking God is unneeded and unwanted. The prodigal son didn't clean up. The woman caught in adultery couldn't clean up. Forget about sewing together fig leaves to cover it up. Adam's and Eve's best embroidery fell desperately short. In this, we exchange deposits of "come as you are" for withdraws of "righteous redemption." Welcome to a new economy! To experience this new nature, we must abandon our present form and attach ourselves completely to Him. The caterpillar must completely give up being a caterpillar to become a butterfly.

From the chrysalis, a butterfly emerges, and from the coffin, a new creature. Paul penned, "Wherefore if any man is in Christ, he is a new creature: the old things are passed away; behold, they are become new" (2 Cor. 5:17 ASV). Often, we interpret Paul's words authoritatively, and we respond to them as conditional. If "any man is in Christ," then "he is a new creature: the old things are passed away." But Paul continues, "behold they *are become* new." The Hebrew translation of the phraseology "are become" is "a prolonged and middle form of a primary verb; to cause to be ('gen'-erate), to become (come into being)."[xxiv] This transmutation is indicative of a process leading to an established end. It would be similar to saying if a caterpillar is in the chrysalis, it's a butterfly: it will no longer act as a caterpillar; everything about it generates into a butterfly. It's an exchange not birthed out of logic and reason, but unconditional love.

Here are a few examples of transformation. Saul was responsible for the death and imprisonment of believers. Despite his best intents to please God, his efforts were nothing more than powdery ruin. In *messy* conditions, Jesus interrupted Saul and engaged with him inclusively, through questions and dialogue. In form, Saul would no longer be in pious agreement with the self-righteous persecution of the church. He was changed from the inside out. Following his transformation, he would confront the Pharisees and face persecution on behalf of the church. The change was so dramatic that when Saul tried to meet with fellow believers, they wavered because they couldn't fathom the change (Acts 9:26). God transformed Saul from a man who persecuted Jesus' believers (Acts 9:13) to a man who would suffer for Jesus (Acts 9:16).

The apostle Mark shares the transformation of a man who lived in the tombs surrounding Gadarenes. Unable to be restrained or controlled, he lived in sorrow, crying and cutting himself with stones (Mark 5:1-5). His ashes consisted of a scourged and lonely life. But like Saul, he had an encounter with Jesus. While others were distant, Jesus came near. Through interacting with Jesus, the tormented man was delivered. A dramatic change followed as the man who was once unkempt became "fully clothed and perfectly sane" (Mark 5:15). The difference was so spectacular that those who witnessed it became afraid. Jesus transformed the man from living amongst dead bones to being commissioned to testify of Him.

A transformation occurred in the life of Peter. The Scriptures record Peter's brazen confession that he would never deny Christ (Matt. 26:35). But shortly after that, Peter denied Christ three times, including an obscenity-laced tirade (Mark 14:66-71). Peter's denial of Christ was an act of cowardice. It was Peter's ashes. And despite his denial, Peter had divine encounters with Jesus after the resurrection (John 21:1-23). And later, being filled with the Holy Spirit (Acts 2:4, 4:8), Peter experienced dramatic change. And once again, those around the change wrestled to understand it. Some thought Peter was part of a drunk crowd (Acts 2:15). Acts 4:13 captures the essence of the transformation experienced in the Earthly Companion blend. The author states, "The members of the council were amazed when they saw the boldness of Peter and John, for they could see that they were ordinary men with no special training in the Scriptures. **They also recognized them as men who had been *with* Jesus**" (Acts 4:13, emphasis mine). They marveled at the dramatic change, and they affirmed that Peter had been *with* Jesus. For the caterpillar, transformation occurs by abiding in the chrysalis; for us, it occurs as we abide with Christ.

| Examples | Ashes | Participative | Transformation |
|----------|-------|---------------|----------------|
| **Saul** | Responsible for death and imprisonment of believers | Jesus engages Saul through question and dialogue on the Damascus Road | From a man who caused Jesus' believers to suffer to one who suffered for the Lord |
| **Man of Gadarenes** | Ostracized Living in tombs Living in sorrow Cutting himself with stones | While others are distant, Jesus is close. He questions the man, and a dialogue ensues. | To a man clothed and sane Commissioned to testify of the great things the Lord had done for him |
| **Peter** | Act of cowardice: the denial of Christ | Despite the denials, Jesus engages Peter through questions and dialogue | Filled with the Holy Spirit. He baptized 3,000 in a single day and spoke boldly. |
| **Moses** | Murderer Sought to be disqualified | Spends time at the burning bush and on Mount Sinai | His face glowed after time with the Lord. He became a deliverer. |

As a final example, Moses yearned to deliver his brothers from slavery. He secretly murdered an Egyptian in defense of an Israelite. Despite Moses' intent, this murderous act did not endear him to his brethren, and he became a fugitive (Ex. 2:15). Forty years later, the Lord invited Moses to return to the scene of the crime. He invited Moses back to Egypt to become the very thing he failed to become on his own: a deliverer. Moses sought disqualification, but eventually, he yielded his failure as ashes and engaged with God through an encounter at a burning bush (Ex. 3). And like Paul, the Man of Gadarenes, and Peter, Moses experienced a dramatic change. Following his time with God at the top of Mount Sinai, Moses came down from God's presence, and his face, like Stephen's, glowed (Ex. 34:29). And once again, those who saw the change were fearful of it (Ex. 34:30). In the context of giving, transformation influences us to give *in response to* God. What has God asked you to abandon personally?

# TRANSFORMATION INTERRUPTED

Like the Commander orientations, focusing only on Earthly Companion behaviors alone can be problematic. King David ignored the law, and he elected to bring the ark of the covenant to Jerusalem based on his relationship with the Lord. But at a bump in the road, when the ark started to fall, the law was ignored, and Uzzah lost his life (2 Sam. 6:7-8). Pleasing the Lord is a combination of obedience (John 14:21) AND walking in relationship with Him. Losing sight of God's authoritative nature is losing sight of His complete nature. When we exhaustively ignore laws and commands, we choose to live in the absence of any order. Subsequently, our self-awareness rots into self-centeredness. We choose to look through the wide end of the funnel, focusing our attention on *our attention*. A benefit of obedience is that it focuses our attention on Someone other than ourselves. It forces us into dependence as we become reliant on the instruction and direction of another.

Another limitation to the Earthly Companion blend occurs if we interrupt God's process of transformation. This interruption occurs if we fail to submit our ashes to the Lord. For three days, Saul endured in darkness, without food or drink. In this solemn coffin of stillness, Saul offered his persecutory past (his ashes). He embraced the process of becoming Paul, the author of roughly one-third of the New Testament.

Contrastingly, Cain failed to submit his failure. In the account of Cain and Abel, we discover that Abel brought an offering of prime rib, with seared gristle, while Cain brought a stale vegetable medley. God preferred Abel's offering and tried to get Cain on the right track. "'Why are you so angry?' the Lord asked Cain. 'Why do you look so dejected? You will be accepted if you do what is right. But if you refuse to do what is right, then watch out! Sin is crouching at the door, eager to control you'" (Gen. 4:6-7). Cain found himself at the decision point of accepting his failure and submitting his ashes. But somewhere between divine feedback and a conversation with his brother, Cain interrupted the process and murdered his brother.

We can also interrupt the process of transformation if we fail to remain in His presence. Scripturally, we observe a change that disrupted Peter's experience of walking on water. Matthew shares, "And when Peter had come down out of the boat, he walked on the water to go to Jesus. But when he saw that the wind was boisterous, he was afraid; and beginning to sink he cried out, saying, 'Lord, save me!'" (Matt. 14:29-30 NKJV). When Peter focused on Jesus, he wasn't distracted, and the process of dramatic change was in full bloom. He was walking on water! But when Peter's focus shifted from Jesus to the sea, he got wet. If we cut open a chrysalis in the middle of the process, we will find something that is no longer a caterpillar but not quite a butterfly. The method of transformation is interrupted. The same is true for us. If our process of remaining in Christ is interrupted, we are not what we were, but not what He's intended us to be. The caterpillar must stay in the chrysalis for the entire transformative period to be complete, just as we must remain *in Christ*. "If anyone does not abide in Me, he is cast out as a branch and is withered" (John 15:6 NKJV). The caterpillar never becomes a butterfly without abandoning all.

## NO NEED TO WALK ALONE

The transition from Heavenly Commander to Earthly Companionship crosses the chasm of living for God to walking with God in our present situations. Along this road, we discover how to hold on to God and let everything else go. Independent of our health, finances, friendships, and goals, we learn to abide in Him, and He abides in us. And as a close encounter of the divine kind begins, our experience moves beyond a dramatic change into an inclusive ***relation-***

*ship* with a risen Christ. John's words echo, "So the Word became human and made his home among us. He was full of unfailing love and faithfulness" (John 1:14). And we experience firsthand the meaning of His name, *Emmanuel or "God with us."* Our transformation experience promotes our **relationship** with God, as we yield more of ourselves to Him.z

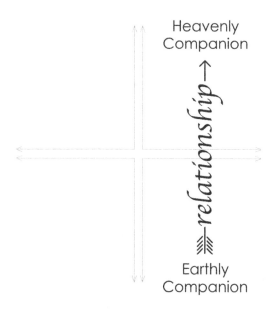

This maturation is much like a child who has been belittled at school. The child has tried repeatedly to defend himself, thinking, "*If I take a different route to school, then they will leave me alone.*" Or "*If I do well on this next paper, then I will be accepted.*" Despite these self-initiated efforts, the offenders still demean the young student. He thinks to himself, "*This would never have happened to my brother.*" He begins to consider, *"What would my brother do?"* He tries to act like his big brother. He deepens his voice. He practices saying things his brother says. On one occasion, he even wears his brother's jacket. These slight adjustments are occasionally helpful, but he is still bullied. Eventually, he grows so frustrated that he can no longer keep the matter to himself.

He comes home crying and tells his brother everything. He shares how he feels. He asks his older brother what he should do. Eventually, he asks his older brother to walk with him to school the following day. The loving brother gladly accepts the invitation. He accompanies his younger sibling to school the next day. On the way there, they encounter the bullies. The bullies don't immediately recognize the connection between the two. They begin to make fun of their classmate, but the older brother intervenes. The relationship between their classmate and the newcomer becomes apparent. The bullies stumble over their words, and sheepish glances replace their threatening actions. Word gets out, "He has a big brother." In class, the abusive jeers of fellow students cease in the shadowing presence of his older brother. The young student is overwhelmed with joy. He rejoices all the way home.

Replaying the victories over and over again, the younger brother excitingly relives the day with his friends. "You should have seen the look on their faces," he excitedly shares. "They didn't say ANYTHING, and guess who was nice to me?" he exclaims. He tells his story repeatedly about how his older brother saved the day. The next morning, the young student gets ready for school, but his brother is nowhere to be found. His heart skips a beat. He feigns sick, but his parents aren't fooled. When he can procrastinate no more, he sighs, grabs his books, and steps outside. Only to find his brother waiting for him, smiling. "You never have to go to school alone," he says. And the younger brother never looks or acts the same again. He no longer focuses on his safety; his big brother is near. He spends less time trying to act like his brother and more time with his brother. And each day, he finds himself focusing less on himself and spending more time learning from his big brother.

The meaning of this allegory is apparent, as we experience the Earthly Companion nature of our divine Creator. We discover that He never intended for us to be alone. Our relationship was not meant to be only reflective of a King and His servants. God sees us as His children and joint-heirs. Jesus sees us as His bride. And like the parable above, He excitedly gets *involved* in our messes. The young brother experienced dramatic change because he came to the end of himself. He stopped trying to change himself and stopped going to school alone. Once accompanied, he no longer looked or acted the same. In transformation, like the younger brother, we come to the end of ourselves. We allow God our Father and Jesus our Lord to lead the change within us. We recognize Jesus as Emmanuel! Like Peter, our cowardice turns to boldness, or like Saul, our ruthlessness turns to compassion. Our Creator is ever-present with us.

Contrary to conventional wisdom, we are not racing to independence. We discover our maturity *in*-dependence, a state of being in "dependence" on our Lord. God accompanies us, we celebrate the success of our relationship, and we naturally testify about all the things God has done for us.

We celebrate provision, but we don't focus on provision. We rejoice about success even though we're not talking to Him about being successful. We find ourselves looking more like Him because we spend more time *with* Him. And as we do, we become *thirsty*. Remember David's words, "As the deer longs for streams of water, / so I long for you, O God. / I thirst for God, the living God. / When can I go and stand before him?" (Psalm 42:1-2). As we experience His presence, our relationship grows roots beneath the surface, and we experience an inner change. Productivity gives us the belief to conform. And conformity causes us to look like Christ while showing us our limitations and our need to transform. But transformation changes our nature and initiates a thirst for *relationship* with the Lord. It's a thirst that causes us to want to go with Him wherever He goes, even to a cross.

# RECAP

- The Earthly Companion blend is working *with* God amid our earthly circumstances.

- In this blend, God allows us to express our doubts and concerns.

- Here, we interact with Divinity not merely as King or Commander but as Friend and Comforter.

- Participative behavior creates nuanced, personal experiences going beyond conformity.

- God engages us through heuristics, not only memorizing and reciting Scriptures.

- Through the Earthly Companion blend, we discover God in ways that are specific to us.

- In this Abandonment Response, God drives the change. In walking *with* our Creator, we transform.

- The caterpillar is completely encapsulated in the chrysalis. We must become surrounded and insulated *in* Jesus.

- Transformation occurs from the inside out in His regenerative process.

- An Earthly Companion transformation contains three critical elements: dying (an exchange of ashes), presence (a participative encounter), and a dramatic change (in form, appearance, or character).

- In the context of giving, transformation influences us to *give in response to* God.

- Key biblical stories: Paul as a Pharisee (Phil. 3:5-6), Saul's conversion to Paul (Acts 9), Stephen's death (Acts 7), Paul's letters (Rom. 12:2, 2 Cor. 5:17, Gal. 6:15), Man of Gadarenes (Mark 5), Peter (Matt. 26, Mark 14, John 21), Moses (Ex. 2, 3:7-4:17)

CHAPTER 5

# FOURTH BLEND: HEAVENLY COMPANION

## ILLICIT SEX AND INTIMACY

In debate after debate, the Pharisees found themselves on the losing end of altercations with Jesus. He rebuffed their objections with impenetrable resolve. In the face of death threats, Jesus spoke bravely, taunting the Pharisees, saying, "You will search for me but not find me. And you cannot go where I am going" (John 7:34). His bold, unapologetic words led the unindoctrinated to believe. The scribes' officers failed to capture Jesus, explaining their actions by saying, "We have never heard anyone speak like this!" (John 7:46). The Pharisees' grip was beginning to slip. The people were choosing to believe in Jesus, despite the wishes of the Jewish elite. Even fellow Pharisees, like Nicodemus, were coming to the defense of this Galilean prophet. After another bad day, the Pharisees broke for the night. They continued to contemplate how they might derail this unforeseen King.

The following morning, Jesus arrives early to the temple. As always, He attracts a crowd. For the Pharisees, the new day brings a new scheme. While Jesus is teaching a group of early-morning followers, the scribes and Pharisees interrupt the lesson. They begin strong-arming a single disheveled woman. Half-dressed and shamed, the woman is surrounded by her accusers. The Pharisees forcibly direct her into the middle of the assembly to disclose her illicit act. "'Teacher,' they said to Jesus, 'this woman was caught in the act of adultery'" (John 8:4). They are looking for an order to kill her, and they want it from Jesus' lips.

The Pharisees continue, "The law of Moses says to stone her. What do you say?" (John 8:5). It appears to be the perfect trap. It seems the Pharisees have cornered Jesus between two mutually exclusive decisions. If Jesus orders them to stone her, His hands will be blooded and His reputation tainted. The compassionate, healing Messiah that many had come to believe in would have ordered the death of this defenseless woman, too closely resembling the Pharisees in judgment. But if He doesn't authorize stoning her, He will appear to condone her sinful act and neglect the law of Moses. Wasn't it just the day prior when Jesus proclaimed in John 7:19, "Moses gave you the law, but none of you obeys it!"? And now sprawled before Him is a woman who has broken the law of Moses. Her punishment is explicit: death by stoning. The Pharisees set the trap to reduce the distinction between themselves and Jesus. Either choice will reward the Pharisees with a long-anticipated win.

The prosecution rests and awaits Jesus' judgment. Instead, Jesus ignores their indictments. Unrushed and unfazed, He begins to write in the dust. They press Him for a decision regarding the woman's fate. Their entrapment appears flawless. All they need is Jesus' response. They incessantly demand He weigh in with a verdict. The accusers wait. The mob, with stones in hand, waits. His early-morning students wait. And the accused woman, exposed and vulnerable, also waits. Jesus finally stands up and says, "All right, but let the one who has never sinned throw the first stone!" (John 8:7). And then He turns His attention away from the crowd and goes back to writing on the ground.

In an unanticipated twist, Jesus doesn't choose option A (stone her) or option B (let her go) as they contrived. He chooses option C (he who has never sinned toss the first stone). His judgment is clear and direct. The stoning is authorized. All they need is a single sinless accuser. But as Jesus' words reach their consciences, conviction takes hold. Each member of the murderous mob evaluates their lives against the judgment. Each one considers their righteousness and find themselves imperfect. And in acknowledgment of their own sinful nature, each one *walks away.* A pattern ensues as they walk away: it begins with the oldest to the youngest. The mob's dismissal is not random but linear. First, the grandfather leaves, then the father. Lastly, the grandson walks away. Uncle, before nephew; older brother, before younger sibling, they go. This ordered progression leaves the youngest last to leave. And the less aged accusers are left with the permanent memory of their indignant elders reduced from accusers to acquitters when faced with their sinfulness.

One by one, everyone leaves. Jesus barely notices. Only the accused woman and Jesus remain. Jesus rises and asks the woman, "'Where are your accusers? Didn't even one of them condemn you?' 'No, Lord,' she said'" (John 8:10-11). Not one is left to accuse. Not one is left to convict. Not one is left to throw a stone. And the imperfect woman in her most imperfect state is left alone with an all-perfect Lord. Jesus has every right to condemn her, but instead, He speaks to her, saying, "Neither do I. Go and sin no more" (John 8:11).


# HEAVENLY COMPANION NATURE EXPLAINED


In the Heavenly Companion blend, we participate with God regarding celestial aspirations. God interacts with us like a Bridegroom with His Bride. From Adam and Eve walking in God's presence to Jesus, *Emmanuel*, the Word becoming flesh and dwelling amongst us, to the Holy Spirit, *The Comforter*, dwelling within us. This blend goes beyond just our earthly conditions, focusing on the world to come, although the circumstances are often messy like the woman cast at Jesus' feet. Consequently, transparency and vulnerability characterize this blend. Jesus never talked to the adulterous woman specifically about adultery. God's Heavenly Companion nature extends beyond if-then thinking. It allows for relational unconditionality. In this case, Jesus told the woman to go and sin no more after He told her that He didn't condemn her. His response was unconditional, even though the scribes and Pharisees tried to get Him to act conditionally.

This aspect of God's nature introduces a blend birthed out of stillness, silence, and solitude. Like the caterpillar, after we beat our newly formed wings against the walls of a spiritual chrysalis, we too emerge changed. Within this aspect of God's nature, we experience Christ as joint-heirs. Paul explains,

> So you have not received a spirit that makes you fearful slaves. Instead, you received God's Spirit when he adopted you as his own children. Now we call him, "Abba, Father." For his Spirit joins with our spirit to affirm that we are God's children. And since we are his children, we are his heirs. In fact, together with Christ we are heirs of God's glory. But if we are

to share his glory, we must also share his suffering. (Rom. 8:15-17)

In the last blend, we discussed abandoning everything for Christ. This blend affirms us as joint-heirs of Christ, a role that is unearned and undeserved. This blend exemplifies the proximity of a continued journey as we continue to draw near to the Lord, and He continues to draw near to us. We grow more united with the Lord. In this aspect of His nature, we grow inseparable and indwelled. By responding to His Spirit, God leads us to a place where we are unified and inseparable from Him.

In God's Heavenly Companion nature, communication is more collaborative. It resembles His conversation with Abraham before the destruction of Sodom and Gomorrah. "'Should I hide my plan from Abraham?' the Lord asked" (Gen. 18:17). The conversation is indicative of a relationship that allows for open discussion, even regarding the Lord's plans. Upon hearing the Lord's intentions, Abraham questioned the Lord, saying, "Will you sweep away both the righteous and the wicked?" (Gen. 18:23). Like an adopted son and joint-heir, Abraham bargained with the Lord regarding Sodom's destruction. And the Lord conceded several times to Abraham's negotiated terms.

Within the Heavenly Companion blend, pleasing God is personal and specific. At times, it may deviate from traditional norms. Conventionally speaking, the adulterous woman's sin would have resulted in her death. Jesus was pleased to let her go and instruct her to live differently. Remarkably, we never hear anything else about this woman again. But we know she had an experience with the living God. I suppose that's all we need to know. As we grow in our relationship with the Lord, to please Him is to know Him. Despite our faults and shortcomings, the Creator of the world wants to share Himself entirely with us and for us to share ourselves entirely with Him. In this uncanny communion, God interacts with us, extending freewill without limiting His authority.

The Heavenly Companion blend is an **Authenticity** Response. The word authentic means "made or done the same way as an original" or "true to one's own personality, spirit, or character."[xxv] Life is interwoven with our Creator's ever-constant desire to share in a relationship with us. Not a uniform, formal, scripted relationship, but a unique, personal, form-fitted one. God shared with Jeremiah, "I knew you before I formed you in your mother's womb" (Jer. 1:5). Jesus shared, "The very hairs on your head are all numbered" (Matt. 10:30). Each case reveals the Lord's desire to interact with us personally. This sentiment is exhaustively observed in God's distinct and specific interactions with Adam, Enoch, Abraham, Isaac, Jacob, Moses, David, many other biblical characters, and extending to us today.

| | |
|---|---|
| *Focus* | Walking "with" Jesus toward the world to come |
| *Context* | Heavenly minded unconditionality |
| *Roles* | Joint-heirs with Christ |
| *Communication* | Collaborative, open discussion |
| *Proximity* | Unified and inseparable |
| *Choice* | Freewill |
| *Pleasing God* | Knowing Him |

# THE IMPORTANCE OF INTIMACY

The aim of this Authenticity Response is **intimacy** *with* God. Intimacy is defined as "close familiarity or friendship."[xxvi] Like a loving parent or affectionate spouse, giving in this context is *giving just because.* Scripturally, this divine intimacy is evident in Enoch's relationship with God. He took quiet walks with God until he was eventually translated into God's actual presence, surpassing even death. In writing to the Corinthians, Paul said: "For now we see in a mirror, darkly; but then face to face" (1 Cor. 13:12 ASV). A time is coming when our understanding will no longer be obscured. We will stand before the Lord, face to face, eye to eye, unimpeded, and without separation. Our later will resemble our beginning where Adam and Eve stood before the Lord naked and unafraid. We can look forward to a heavenly outcome when God speaks to us as He spoke to Moses, like a friend. Or as He talked to the accused woman, with compassion and forgiveness. And we will know Him even as we are known, with our shortcomings and embarrassments. These intimate moments with the Lord include closeness, warmth, and slowness, and are always personal. Let's examine each of these characteristics.

Closeness is a byproduct of proximity and communion. It requires us to turn toward God, which reduces the distance between Him and us. It is like the prodigal son turning from delicacies meant for pigs and back toward his father's house. The son headed home, and his father met him on the way. Closeness includes responsiveness, as James promised, "Come close to God, and God will come close to you" (James 4:8). In the typical king/servant relationship, distance is maintained through hierarchy, but God is committed to drawing close to us. The ultimate distance between our Creator and us existed when mankind lived in rebellion against Him. Despite those circumstances, God sent His Son to earth (reduced proximity) to die for us so that we may know Him once again (communion restored).

The pinnacle of closeness is unity, a place of oneness, where separation due to distance or ideology is absent. Jesus, in speaking with His Father, shared, "I pray that they will all be one, just as you and I are one—as you are in me, Father, and I am in you" (John 17:21). It's the point of acting and thinking not through conformity, or even transformation, but through relationship and intimacy. As Paul penned, "Let this mind be in you which was also in Christ Jesus"

(Phil. 2:5 NKJV). Unity is closeness to the point of being inseparable, inextricably connected with our Lord, unconditionally. Paul described this indivisible unity to the church at Rome saying,

> And I am convinced that nothing can ever separate us from God's love. Neither death nor life, neither angels nor demons, neither our fears for today nor our worries about tomorrow—not even the powers of hell can separate us from God's love...indeed, nothing in all creation will ever be able to separate us from the love of God that is revealed in Christ Jesus our Lord. (Rom 8:38-39)

The Lord's aim is for us to be inseparable, living in divine unity with Him.

The second characteristic of intimacy is warmth. One biblical author shared, "Likewise, two people lying close together can keep each other warm. But how can one be warm alone?" (Ecclesiastes 4:11). It's difficult to generate heat on our own and challenging to express warmth from a distance. Warmth is a derivative of closeness. We can experience it through temperature or a simple act of kindness. A first responder covers a victim with a blanket to make them feel more comfortable. This act of kindness covers, protects, and begins to restore the sufferer mentally and physically. Even in humanity's eviction from the garden, God clothed Adam and Eve with coats of skins. It was an act of kindness that covered, protected, and began a process of reconciliation.

Warmth communicates kindheartedness that thaws the heart of the recipient and the giver. And where the Father offered furs in the garden, Jesus offered an unprecedented Comforter on His way back to Heaven. "And I will pray the Father, and he shall give you another Comforter, that he may be with you for ever" (John 14:16 ASV). As the ultimate source of warmth that covers, protects, and restores us, the Lord's Spirit fills us. And like the caterpillar that changes from the inside out, the Holy Spirit indwells us. It ignites an inner change that reflects outwardly.

At times, warmth is created through friction. Like two pieces of wood in contact but moving in opposite directions, friction induces heat and creates sparks. Consider Jesus' dialogue with the Gentile woman seeking deliverance for her daughter. Begging for mercy, she acknowledges the lordship of Jesus. She cries, "Have mercy on me, O Lord, Son of David! For my daughter is possessed by a demon that torments her severely" (Matt. 15:22). At first, Jesus ignores her plea for help. *Friction.* Her voice goes unacknowledged, but it is not unheard. In her parental desperation, Jesus' loving disciples respond: "'Tell her to go away,' they said. 'She is bothering us with all her begging'" (Matt. 15:23). The disciples dismiss her. *More friction.* Finally, Jesus acknowledges her, saying, "I was sent only to help God's lost sheep—the people of Israel" (Matt. 15:24). Jesus doesn't say He can't help, but that He wasn't sent to help *her.* Ouch. *More friction.* Despite being ignored, dismissed, and now devalued, her response is incredible.

"She came and worshiped him, pleading again, 'Lord, help me!'" (Matt. 15:25). Jesus responds to her worship, saying, "It isn't right to take food from the children and throw it to the dogs" (Matt. 15:26). It's a demeaning comparison. The Savior of the world likens delivering the woman's daughter to giving the children's food to the dogs. *So much friction.* Jesus' response would bring many to the threshold of offense. How many of us would have grabbed the hand of our child and walked away? Saying to ourselves, "No one is going to talk to me like that!" Friction occurs when objects are moving in opposition to each other. Irrespective of all the reasons to turn *away* from Jesus, the desperate woman continues to press *toward* Him.

Instead of rejecting the canine comparison, she accepts it, saying, "That's true, Lord, but even dogs are allowed to eat the scraps that fall beneath their master's table" (Matt. 15:27). *Friction, friction, friction, friction, spark!* Upon hearing the mother's response, Jesus affectionally says, "'Dear woman…your faith is great. Your request is granted.' And her daughter was instantly healed" (Matt. 15:28). This mom endured being ignored, dismissed, devalued, and demeaned. As a result, she experienced a warmth that covered her daughter, and Jesus experienced a great enduring faith. Friction ignited warmth!

Slow cooked. Slow roasted. There's something about slowness that influences intimacy. It's the essence of waiting. My wife and I recently attended a concert in Dallas, Texas. Whenever I visit Dallas, I like to try out a different barbeque spot. We followed the suggestion of the concierge from our hotel, and the place was phenomenal. We ate like royalty and had the pleasure of speaking with the grill master. He starts as early as 4 a.m., but the result is well worthwhile.

Too often, slowness requires more time than we are willing to give. Like Abraham and Sarah waiting for the promised son, we grow impatient in our waiting and, at times, produce something unintended. Slowness develops patience, and patience produces perfection (James 1:4). We learn a lot about ourselves when facing delayed expectations. Do we remain focused? How's our temperament? Can we stay deliberate in our decision-making? Waiting is where eagerness and expectancy meet. They create the tumultuous waters that batter hope, mold endurance, and foster restraint. If we wait appropriately, we are rewarded with rejoicing without regret as our hope is fulfilled. Please don't equate my understanding of the value of waiting with me actually waiting well. In terms of slow roasting, let's just say I've eaten my share of undercooked meat.

Slowness may relate to the pace of movement, but it can also refer to our forethought before acting. Our Creator demonstrates a slow and deliberate approach toward the needs of His children. At times it's explained but not always understood. God allows our situations to season us. He tenderizes our hearts over periods of waiting, like the woman suffering from the issue of blood (twelve years), Joseph carrying a dream (seventeen years), Abraham waiting for the promised child (twenty-five years), or the children of Israel in the wilderness (forty years). Similar to a master chef, He receives the desires of a hungry crowd with patience, which opens the door to perfection. In slowness, we are fully immersed in the experience and more reliant upon the Lord.

The Master Designer has committed Himself to the art of slowness, and it leads us to perfection, completion, and satisfaction. Momentarily, contrast this with authoritative "here and now" or "cause and effect" thinking. Immediacy often lacks substance. Adam Pasick published an article that explored the collapse of quickly built apartment buildings in response to China's population boom.[xxvii] The absence of slowness, like a city too quickly erected, produces a skyline not afforded sufficient time to settle. These poorly crafted structures serve as cautionary tales as they collapse under the feeblest of winds. It is difficult to build things that last quickly. This art of deliberation and intentionality is not only relevant to the successful design of a building, but it is crucial to the construction of our character.

When we react in the moment, we live quick to speak, slow to listen, and quick to anger. Absent of slowness, we become reactive and inconsistent—our lives resembling flickering lights, failing to see past the moment. We fail to learn how to endure, and we lose the advantage of momentum. Eventually, our lives resemble an embattled swimmer, shipwrecked and abandoned, desperately battling the current in hopes of reaching the distant shore. We swim. We drift. We tire. We drown. Our daily diet erodes to nothing more than a collection of TV dinners and microwaveables, lacking nutrients and taste. The fast-food stalwart McDonald's recognized the need for slowness, with the introduction of their *new* beef Quarter Pounder burger cooked ONLY on arrival. They slowed things down to improve their quality and to make the meal a bit more *personal.*

Closeness, warmth, and slowness have physical and emotional connotations. Unlike the others, *personal* is unified in its application. It's independent of being characterized as physical or emotional because its very nature is individualized and encompassing. There are areas on the body that are inappropriate to touch without consent and topics of discussion that are off-limits without permission. When things are *personal,* specific approval is required. Personal is the final step to intimacy.

Consider the intimate moments we share. The aged and wrinkled face of a man gazing into the eyes of his wife. Or a young father reclining shirtless on the couch, while his infant sleeps to the beat of his heart. These intimate scenarios rarely observe general prescriptive patterns. The very nature of intimacy is personal. Yet, many of us only endeavor to *know* God in the presence of others. Our expressions of praise only occur at church. And our prayers are only fashioned in "repeat after me" recitations. To this end, Jesus warned, "When you pray, don't be like the hypocrites who love to pray publicly on street corners and in the synagogues where everyone can see them" (Matt. 6:5). Alternatively, Jesus urged us to engage with our Father with a more intimate and personal approach. Jesus said,

But when you pray, go away by yourself, shut the door behind you, and pray to your Father in private. Then your Father, who sees everything, will reward you.

When you pray, don't babble on and on as the Gentiles do. They think their prayers are answered merely by repeating their words again and again. (Matt. 6:6-7)

Jesus describes a prayer setting that is isolated, secret, meaningful, and original. We wouldn't expect a good husband to only speak to his wife in the presence of others but live in silence behind closed doors. Nor would we expect a loving groom to exclusively express his love for his bride through unoriginal collective repetitions, like lines from a play. When a caring mother gazes into the eyes of her child, what she speaks is often spontaneous, unique, and personal. Real intimacy is evident in its own nature. If the predominance of our connections with Christ are general and rule-based, how can we *know* Him personally? Let's revisit Jesus' actions in the case of the woman caught in adultery through these four elements.

*Closeness.* Despite being interrupted by the situation, Jesus allowed Himself to get actively involved. While others sought to distance themselves, *it takes two to commit adultery,* Jesus stayed *close.* Throughout this account, Jesus never distanced Himself from the woman in proximity or from her sinfulness. Conversely, Jesus defended the woman through *closeness.* He connected the woman's sinful act to the sinfulness of her accusers. "Let the one who has never sinned throw the first stone!" (John 8:7). They found themselves no longer detached. They could not remain separated in piousness, but like the woman, they were exposed. Their cold, hardened hearts grew introspective. And in unwanted empathy, one by one, they walked away. And when everyone was gone, Jesus was still within earshot.

*Warmth.* Like God blanketing the first couple with furs in place of leaves, Jesus protected the woman. Jesus expressed warmth through acts of kindness. When standing at odds with a cold, self-righteous mob, Jesus chose silence, while others flurried accusations. He decided to defend, while others elected to attack. He opted to forgive, while others chose judgment. Consider the inherent conflict between the perfection of Jesus and the fallibility of the woman, presumably on her worst hair day. Heading in different directions, the lives of Jesus and the woman collided. And like two pieces of metal struck together, the abrasiveness of this dichotomy ignited unconditional love. Jesus created warmth through closeness, kindness, and friction.

*Slowness.* Writing, speaking, then back to writing, Jesus never rushed. He didn't rush the accusers through their accusations. He gave the mob time to gather their stones. Despite a rancorous crowd that was out for blood, Jesus wasn't unsettled. Not rushing to the woman's aid with quick retorts, He was deliberate and methodical. Slow to speak, yet quick to listen. Jesus slow-cooked the situation, valuing every word, every allegation, and every action. And at His response, the angry accusers didn't disperse quickly. They scattered thoughtfully and methodically, one by one and ordered. God's nature was exhibited, even in the faultfinders' dismissal. Jesus kept it on slow, and the stones were never thrown.

*Personal*. Jesus never lost sight of the woman through the view of the crowd. His words were individually directed and specific. To the publicly humiliated and condemned, Jesus conveyed a personal message: "I don't condemn you either. Live differently." What an example. Can you recall a time the Lord simply remained with you, despite your mess and sinfulness? I can.

## PURPOSELY INTIMATE

Like the other blends, exclusive use of the Heavenly Companion blend can be destructive. Much like conformity isn't always positive, intimacy isn't always authentic. True intimacy is consistent with our God-given purpose. We don't know what drove the adulterous woman into the arms of a man who was not her husband. Maybe it was loneliness. Perhaps, her lover made her feel valued. But unlike authentic intimacy, false intimacy is like drinking to relieve our thirst but never feeling quenched. In many cases, our craving intensifies. Delilah provided Samson with intimate moments. But those moments were superficial because they debilitated

Samson's ability to perform his purpose, which was to war against the Philistines.

Consider how protective Jesus was of His purpose. Jesus asks His disciples, "Who do people say that the Son of Man is?" (Matt. 16:14). They answer, "Some say John the Baptist, some say Elijah, and others say Jeremiah or one of the other prophets" (Matt. 16:14). The public didn't discern who Jesus was, so Jesus asks the disciples, "But who do you say I am?" (Matt. 16:15). Peter gets it right, "You are the Messiah, the Son of the living God" (Matt. 16:16). Jesus responds, "You are blessed, Simon son of John, because my Father in heaven has revealed this to you. You did not learn this from any human being" (Matt. 16:17). Jesus begins to share with the disciples that His purpose would require Him to suffer and die in Jerusalem. In a well-meaning moment, Peter rebukes Jesus: "'Heaven forbid, Lord,' he said. 'This will never happen to you!'" (Matt. 16:22). Immediately, Jesus reprimands Peter, saying, "Get away from me, Satan! You are a dangerous trap to me. You are seeing things merely from a human point of view, not from God's" (Matt. 16:23).

Jesus took misunderstanding His purpose very seriously. False intimacy is deceptive. It's not designed to bolster our purpose, but to usurp it. Salt water is water, but its chemical makeup is not designed for human hydration. In fact, it intensifies our dehydration. The pursuit of intimacy, apart from authenticity, can be debilitating. Where we meet God in our purpose-filled design, we find "a triple-braided cord is not easily broken" (Eccl. 4:12).

Another limitation of the Authenticity Response is only having a Companion blend view of God. In this case, our *Christianity* is based on our experiences with the Lord, without regard for scriptural consistency. Our personal freedom becomes a gateway to bondage, as we subjugate His authority to our preferences. Through closeness, we take for granted His holiness and become relaxed in our response to Him. We allow truth to become lost in debate, and God's commands become open to our own interpretation. Always open for discussion, but rarely committed to study, we participate in the body of Christ at our discretion. Seeing ourselves only as friends of God's, and seldomly as servants, we become gods unto ourselves. Within this unbalanced approach, we often respond with "I'll take it under advisement" instead of "Thy will be done."

On several occasions, Peter demonstrated an unbalanced Companion approach. For instance, Peter's rebuke of Jesus regarding the crucifixion (Matt. 16:22). Or his suggestions during the transfiguration to build a tabernacle (Matt. 17:4). Also Peter's bold confession that he'd rather die than betray Christ (Matt. 26:33). Each is an example of the disciple comfortably, yet mistakenly, involving himself in the decision-making process with the Son of God. In the first example, Jesus rebuked Peter. In the second, God spoke in authority, saying, "This is my dearly loved Son, who brings me great joy. Listen to him," and Peter falls on his face, terrified (Matt. 17:5). In the third example, Peter was convicted at the moment by the glance of Jesus. None of the blends are exclusive. We mature as we experience God according to His nature and not according to our preference of His nature.

# PURPOSE-FILLED CONNECTION

One day, a young man is on a date with a young lady. They go out for lunch at a local restaurant. They order a Dr. Pepper, salad, and a pizza topped with mushrooms and pepperoni. Thirty minutes pass, and (as the French say) the pièce de résistance arrives. Bowing their heads, they hold hands and say grace. After the "amen," the young man looks in her direction and says, "Everyone loves pizza…" Is this personal? *Maybe, maybe not.* But what if I said that the young lady used to eat at this pizzeria as a child? She and her dad would make the occasional stop on the way home from school just to talk. Many moments of warmth and closeness filled this pizzeria. And every time, following the grace, her dad would look at her, smile, and say, "Jackie, everyone loves pizza." Shortly after their last impromptu daddy-daughter date, her dad passed away unexpectedly. She shared her fondness for the restaurant as the source of some of her most cherished moments. So, the young man took Jackie out on an unexpected date, for a mushroom and pepperoni pizza, in the place of her fondest memories. Before eating, they said grace, and he looked into her eyes and said, "Jackie, everyone loves pizza." *Personal*? Absolutely, because personal moments incorporate our *uniqueness* to create distinctive, private moments. Moments that convey that we're being listened to *and* being heard. Moments that go beyond being looked at to being seen. Moments that remind us of what it feels like to be known.

The Heavenly Companion blend is the peak of a journey beginning in belief, growing through humility, strengthening into a relationship, and culminating with us residing in Him.

Let's revisit the story of Martha and Mary. They both loved Jesus, but they demonstrated their love very differently. Mary sat at Jesus' feet and listened to His every word. Luke recorded the event saying, "Martha was distracted by the big dinner she was preparing" (Luke 10:40). It is interesting that she is described as *distracted*, given the responsibilities of hosting. But when Jesus is present, everything else is nothing more than a distraction.

Many of us, like Martha, are distracted. On many occasions, we gather to worship but focus on other things instead of the "guest of honor." We are careful about so many things, but only one thing is needful: being with Him. And like the story, our competing demands may be the needs or expectations of others. But there is only one requirement, only one place where we should take up residence. And Mary found it at the feet of Jesus, a *purpose-filled connection with the Author of life*. Mary chose it, and so can we.

Residing in the Lord requires us to focus on Him, despite the noise of competing voices. There are the opinions of others, the suggestions of the well-meaning, the barbs from haters, the consensus of the culture, and the voice of our own self-conscious. And through the noise of various sentiments, God expects us to know Him and recognize His voice (John 10:14).

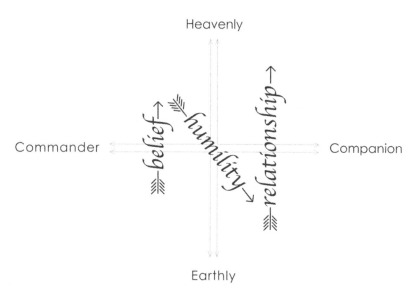

# RECAP

- The Heavenly Companion, also known as the Authenticity Response, is shown when we participate (true to our personality) with God toward celestial aspirations.

- Heavenly participation is characterized by two-way communication.

- From Adam and Eve walking in God's presence to Jesus, *Emmanuel*, the Word becoming flesh and dwelling amongst us, to the Holy Spirit, *The Comforter*, dwelling within us— God's intent from the beginning has been to *know* us and to be *known* by us.

- The outcome of the Heavenly Companion blend is to know God and be known by Him.

- Intimate moments include closeness, warmth, and slowness and are always personal.

- The Lord's aim is for us to be inseparable, living in divine unity with God.

- Warmth is a derivative of closeness. It can be experienced as temperature or as an act of kindness.

- At times, warmth is created through friction.

- Slowness may relate to the pace of movement, but it can also allude to our considerations and forethought before acting.

- Personal is individualized and encompassing.

- Pursuing intimacy without an appreciation for God's Commander nature can lead to false intimacy. True intimacy is consistent with our *purpose*.

- Key biblical stories: Abraham (Gen. 18), Gentile mother (Matt. 15), Peter (Matt 16) and the adulterous woman (John 8)

CHAPTER

6

# BALANCED & COMPLETE

Heavenly

**Heavenly Commander**
Adjustment (theme)
Conformity (outcome)

**Heavenly Companion**
Authenticity (theme)
Intimacy (outcome)

Commander

Companion

**Earthly Commander**
Awareness (theme)
Productivity (outcome)

**Earthly Companion**
Abandonment (theme)
Transformation (outcome)

Earthly

## A SON, A SIBLING, AND A FATHER

A wealthy landowner had two sons. The younger son knew that he would receive his inheritance following his father's death. But he didn't want to wait. He wanted the pleasures associated with riches now! So he asked his father for his share of the inheritance, prematurely. Surprisingly to most, despite the inherent conflict, his father conceded and divided his youngest son's estate from his brother's. The young man left home with his fortune in search of something more. There was no shortage of things on which to spend his money, but eventually, he found himself financially exhausted. As life would have it, his funds ran out about the time a famine ravaged the land.

Without money during a food shortage, the young adventurer began to starve. Broke, but resourceful, he got a job feeding pigs. His hunger became so severe that he considered eating the leftover slop meant to feed the livestock. But he couldn't even get permission from farmers to eat the pigs' food. Eventually, he remembered that his father had employees. And while he was dying of hunger, those employees had leftovers. He headed home barefoot and broken. To his surprise, his Father recognized him long before he reached home. Luke recounts, "Filled with love and compassion, he [the father] ran to his son, embraced him, and kissed him" (Luke 15:20). His son began to recite an emotional appeal, one which he had practiced for several days, hoping for his father's acceptance; however, love interrupted. The father ordered his servants to *cover him* with the finest robe. In restoration, the father put a ring on the hand of his child and sandals on his bare feet. And instead of a meal fit for a pig, the father honored his son by killing the fattened calf, a meal meant only for the most prestigious occasions and choicest of crowds. Jubilantly, his father proclaimed, "We must celebrate with a feast, for this son of mine was dead and has now returned to life. He was lost, but now he is found" (Luke

15:23-24). I never grow tired of hearing that story, but that's not where it ends. Jesus' parable was a story of siblings.

While one brother prematurely sought his inheritance, the other waited patiently. When the younger brother was squandering his wealth, his older brother was preserving his. As the younger brother frivolously partied, his brother tirelessly labored. One day after working the fields, the sound of distant music, laughter, and dancing caught the faithful brother off guard. It didn't make sense. He asked a servant to tell him the meaning behind the party. They shared with him that his brother had returned home, and his father had killed the fattened calf to celebrate. First, the premature inheritance, then carousing while he worked, and now the fattened calf. The elder brother had had enough. He was irate and wouldn't join the celebration.

The father pleaded with him to join them, but the son refrained. The disheartened son explained,

> All these years I've slaved for you and never once refused to do a single thing you told me to. And in all that time you never gave me even one young goat for a feast with my friends. Yet when this son of yours comes back after squandering your money on prostitutes, you celebrate by killing the fattened calf! (Luke 15:29-30)

The father listened to his offended child and responded, "Look, dear son, you have always stayed by me, and everything I have is yours. We had to celebrate this happy day. For your brother was dead and has come back to life! He was lost, but now he is found!" (Luke 15:31-32).

# TWO DEPARTURES

Jesus was teaching tax collectors and sinners, sometimes even over a meal. The Pharisees and scribes couldn't understand why someone who was supposedly righteous would hang out with the unrighteous. Jesus responded to their concerns by sharing three short stories. The first story was about a lost sheep recovered. The second was about a lost coin found. The third was about a son, a sibling, and a father. Through the story, we discover that both sons at some point left their dad, and the father sought to restore relationship with them both. The story, uniquely crafted by Jesus, is an illustration of a father's love for his two very different sons who went astray.

The story began with the young man demanding his inheritance in pursuit of freedom and independence. Traditionally, he would receive his estate after the death of his father. This custom would allow him to gain knowledge, experience, and understanding as he worked for his father. But the prodigal son hungered for independence. He ignored the opportunity to gain wisdom through restraint and patience. The son overlooked the importance of learning how to be financially disciplined. He ignored the importance of understanding agricultural cycles and how to recognize and prepare for a famine.

The young man discounted the importance of his father's commanding nature in preparing him for his future. Despite his lack of *awareness* and *adjustments* based upon what he'd learn, he wanted his inheritance immediately. The young man opted to leave home and enter an uncertain environment with an abbreviated education. Subsequently, he experienced starvation (the lack of productivity). And possibly due to his lack of maturity, he erroneously sought to conform to the manner of pigs and exchange sonship for servanthood. Sometimes, we strive for freedom and independence at the expense of patience and structure. At times, we underestimate the benefits of God's Commanding nature.

I was surprised by the father's response to his ambitious son's request. In reading this story, I think many of us expect traditional parental norms. We are caught off guard not only by the father saying yes, but even financing the trip. Most of us would not apply the term "loving father" to a dad who allowed his naïve son to move to New York City with bags full of money and a heart filled with ill intentions. We struggle with the incongruence between *our expectations* of God's nature and His actual character, as revealed through His allegory. We expected the father to say no. We expected the father not to give the son his inheritance prematurely. We expected the father to protect his son from himself. Maybe we expected the father to be punitive at his son's return. Overall, we expected the father's approach to be largely rule-based, logical, and ordered. Our partial understanding of God, like the scribes and Pharisees, is seeing only through the lens of God's Earthly Commander nature. This parable introduces us to a more complete view of our Father.

We're not the only ones who misconstrue the Father's nature. Following the prodigal son's failures, he prepared to appeal to his father's authoritarian side. Evaluate how the wasteful son contemplated his situation with a conditional mind-set. He would return home (action), admit his mistake (action) to get food and safety (outcome). Starvation drove his heart to the point of humility and being willing to forfeit his sonship (consequence/outcome). It was a rational solution. But Jesus illustrated the father's grace-filled response. The father forgave his son and covered the stench of countless wrong decisions with his best robe. It was nonsensical, unconditional, and personal. The father reacted to his prodigal son through his companion nature. And Jesus responded to the Pharisees' concerns regarding His behavior with tax collectors and sinners by highlighting the Father's Companion nature.

But this story isn't just about the prodigal son. It's also about a rule-following, compliant older brother. It's about a brother who chose obedience when his sibling chose defiance. A disciplined brother who shepherded his father's wealth, while his younger brother tended to selfish desires. A brother who conformed in expectation of a greater reward. In him, we see the faint resemblance of the rich young ruler: all the right actions for all the wrong reasons. The older brother was comfortable with an ordered and logical approach to living *for* his father. He constructed his relationship with his dad on conditionality. He subjugated himself to his father, as the idea of hierarchy and following rules came naturally to him. But when his brother returned, humbled and disgraced, and his father responded with joy and not judgment, the older brother's countenance changed. And the years of obedience were exposed as dutiful acquiescence. While others celebrated, the older brother was outside and offended. At the return of his lost brother, he was willfully separated from his father, both physically and emotionally.

Part of the beauty of this story is that the same father who ran to meet his wayward son now came out to meet his seemingly righteous one—a point of added importance considering Jesus was addressing the Pharisees. The father begged his son to join them, but he refused. How deceptive is the illusion of obedience based on tradition and custom? When this obedience comes in contact with Divinity, it often falls short. Remember, the rich young ruler didn't *abandon* his riches to join Jesus, and the disgruntled brother did not *abandon* his anger to join his father. On the contrary, the older brother defended his decision to remain outside. His response uncovered the true nature of his corrupted view, and it did not reflect his father's character.

The rich young ruler and the prodigal son's older brother are examples of how we can follow the rules outwardly while being woefully inadequate inwardly. Jesus warned, "Woe to you, scribes and Pharisees, hypocrites! For you are like whitewashed tombs which indeed appear beautiful outwardly, but inside are full of dead men's bones and all uncleanness" (Matt. 23:27 NKJV). Too often, our hearts don't reflect the Father's nature. Our outward actions cover our perverse inward expectations as we do the right things for selfish reasons. We serve God, quid pro quo, to earn "one young goat" to share with our friends. We lose sight of our Father, as we resentfully gaze at our underperforming, yet forgiven, brothers. As a result, we miss out on celebrating God's unconditional love and remain separated with a petrified heart. In the Sermon on the Mount, Jesus warned, "Beware of false prophets who come disguised as harmless sheep but are really vicious wolves" (Matt. 7:15). It's a warning against conforming to the outward appearance, "sheep's clothing," contrasted with the true inner nature of their heart, "ravening wolves" (Matt 7:15 NKJV).

How can we tell whether our obedience is out of duty or relationship? Let's take our time to examine that discussion regarding the difference between false and true prophets. Jesus says,

You can identify them by their fruit, that is, by the way they act. Can you pick grapes from thornbushes, or figs from thistles? A good tree produces good fruit, and a bad tree produces bad fruit. A good tree can't produce bad fruit, and a bad tree can't produce good fruit. So every tree that does not produce good fruit is chopped down and thrown into the fire. Yes, just as you can identify a tree by its fruit, so you can identify people by their actions. (Matt. 7:16-20)

Rationally, this seems simple enough. A good tree produces good fruit. But consider the dialogue that immediately follows, "Not everyone who calls out to me, 'Lord! Lord!' will enter the Kingdom of Heaven. Only those who actually do the will of my Father in heaven will enter" (Matt. 7:21). "Lord, Lord" is an expression of sincere devotion. Jesus explains not everyone who expresses genuine commitment to Him will enter into heaven. He expounds further, "On judgment day many will say to me, 'Lord! Lord! We prophesied in your name and cast out demons in your name and performed many miracles in your name" (Matt. 7:22). In apparent devotion, many will point toward outward evidence: the fruit of prophesying in His name, casting out devils, and other beautiful works. Despite these works being good-natured and scripturally supported, Jesus concludes, "But I will reply, 'I never knew you. Get away from me, you who break God's laws'" (Matt. 7:23).

Jesus' dialogue demonstrates that "good fruit" isn't merely outwardly appealing. I'm sure I'm not the only one who has bitten into an apple that appeared ripe on the outside but was rotten within. It's not just about the works (productivity) or the appearance (conformity), but the existence of authenticity between the outward appearance and the inner heart. Jesus' response to the devoted, yet distorted, is "I *never knew you.*" It's heartbreaking to consider the possibility of being falsely devoted. If we do God-honoring things, but we don't know Him, those works are works of iniquity. Jesus' illustration of the older brother was an indication to the Pharisees that genuine relationship goes beyond obedience or just living *for God*. A real relationship is *knowing Him*.

# THE WHOLENESS OF GOD'S DIVINE NATURE

Independently, each blend is inadequate, but when combined, they give us a more in-depth understanding of the true nature of God. We begin in separation, focusing on little more than our own earthly needs and desires. But with Jesus as Lord, our journey culminates in unity with God, focusing on nothing more than Him. Our relationship with God is not developed in actions alone but in our underlying intent.

It reminds me of a scene in the movie *The Break-Up*.[xxviii] The female protagonist, named Brooke, asks her beau, Gary, to help her wash the dishes. Gary agrees but wants to get some X-Box time in first. Brooke wants to finish the dishes first so that she can go to bed. They bicker back and forth before Gary throws down the controller and says, "Fine!" Discouraged by his lack of support, Brooke refuses Gary's help. They embark upon a comedic discussion of what it is Brooke really wants from him. "I want you to want to do the dishes," she says. Gary quips, "Why would I want to do the dishes?"

Relationship goes beyond compliance. It requires an alignment between actions and motives. Jeremiah exclaimed,

"The human heart is the most deceitful of all things, / and desperately wicked. / Who really knows how bad it is?" (Jer. 17:9). Outwardly, our actions may look honorable, while our intentions are deceptive, dreadful, and disguised. Our relationship with Jesus must go beyond the outer surface and allow our hearts to submit to His will.

In transparency, brokenness, and filth, we come. The first man, woman, marriage, and child all demonstrated considerable lapses in judgment. And today, we too have gazed upon and eaten forbidden delicacies, sweet to the lips but carrying a bitter aftertaste. However, through unconditional love, we undeservedly receive repentance and restoration along with surprise parties, robes, and rings. And in response to our moments of desperation, we experience the Father's love as we make our journey home. Or as we come to terms with celebrating our brother's or our sister's restoration even if they've broken all the rules. We must acknowledge the completeness of our Creator's divine characteristics to interact with Him more fully. Jesus' parable of two sons served as a lesson for the Pharisees and for us today. If we fail to embrace God's complete nature, we can find ourselves on the outside looking in, in this world and the next.

## CONCLUSION

Jesus described himself as the "Lord, even over the Sabbath!" (Matt. 12:8), the Lord over an established rule and practice. He illustrated how this balance, between rule and relationship, was not merely a New Testament phenomenon. Jesus used the example of David eating the showbread, which was against Jewish law. Jesus said, "The Sabbath was made to meet the needs of people, and not people to meet the requirements of the Sabbath" (Mark 2:27). The rule was created for man; man wasn't designed for the rule.

Paul shared, "Now we see things imperfectly, like puzzling reflections in a mirror, but then we will see everything with perfect clarity. All that I know now is partial and incomplete, but then I will know everything completely, just as God now knows me completely" (1 Cor. 13:12). Consider the imagery: We see things like puzzling reflections in a mirror, distorting our view. As a result, we have a partial understanding. An unbalanced view of God's nature is like that cloudy mirror, causing us to see Him partially. As a result, we fail to realize that God's divine nature is equally Commander and Companion.

A distorted view of God—and, consequently, a contorted view of ourselves—prevents us from reflecting His glory. God created us in His image. He designed us to reflect His nature. A balanced walk *with* the Lord more accurately mirrors His image. It reveals His Earthly Commander nature, as the Lord meets the Earthly needs of others through us. He may use us to feed the starving or shelter the homeless. He may heal the sick through us, supernaturally, or by just giving someone a ride to get their meds. In exemplifying God's

Earthly Commander nature, we bring awareness to His awesomeness and cause the unbelieving to *believe.*

As we walk balanced *with* the Lord, we echo His Heavenly Commander nature as we respond to the question, "What must I do to be saved?" We discuss belief in Jesus, our repentance, and we testify to the adjustments we've made to conform to the image of Christ. Our very lives serve as examples of righteousness, self-righteousness, failure, and repentance. Ultimately, we reveal a true humility within us and uncover our need for a closer walk *with* Him.

A balanced walk also reflects God's Earthly Companion nature. Like Eli the prophet, we may help others interact with the Lord *personally* by teaching them to respond to the Lord saying, "Speak, Lord, your servant is listening" (1 Sam. 3:9). Our lives attest to the role of abandoning everything in order to *know* Him. And our testimonies illustrate the distinction between self-led conformity and God-led transformation. The butterfly-like nature in each of us is being revealed solely by His grace and unconditional nature.

Ultimately, a balanced walk will reveal God's Heavenly Companion nature. As we draw near to God, and our relationship with Him tightens, we begin to reflect the authentic nature of our Lord, the life of one walking in complete unity and oneness with God. Echoing Jesus' hope, "I pray that they will all be one, just as you and I are one—as you are in me, Father, and I am in you" (John 17:21).

By growing in our understanding of God, we can gain a better understanding of His authored intent in creating us.

We begin to understand our purpose more clearly. Jeremiah shared the words of the Lord, "I knew you before I formed you in your mother's womb" (Jer. 1:5). Like a blacksmith creating an instrument, God formed us with intent. In the New Testament, Paul reaffirmed our design when he shared with the Philippians, "For God is working in you, giving you the desire and the power to do what pleases him" (Phil. 2:13). God has worked into us desire and power. We have been designed on and with purpose.

Too often, we resist the One who loves us and opt for poorly fitting clothes to cover our nakedness. We choose logic in place of incongruence. It makes sense, and that's the problem. We let go of the pursuit of the extraordinary, in exchange for the ordinary. And we find ourselves grievingly walking away from Jesus as part of a recurring story from Genesis to the present moment. Many of us have fallen short because we've chosen not to come and follow. And this decision leads us away from a mysterious, adventurous, responsive life with a heart intertwined with our Lord.

My mom asked me the other day, "When you talk about seeking God's presence, what do you mean?" I smiled as I reminisced about one such occasion. A few years ago, I traveled to Jacksonville, Florida, with my youngest daughter. It was a two-day event with a concert the first night. We were excited to hear some of our favorite Christian artists. We flew in from Atlanta on Friday evening and immediately headed to the church hosting the event. We arrived before everything got started. The master of ceremonies excitedly yelled, "How are you doing, Jacksonville?" The music was great! We enjoyed singing songs of praise to God along with the featured artist and the congregation. It was great!

The next morning, the workshop started at 10 a.m. The first session began with worship. That day, the master of ceremonies, in a very nonchalant, straightforward fashion, introduced the worship leader. She wasn't a featured artist. I don't recall her name. She took the microphone, bowed her head, and uttered something like, "Lord, we humbly come to worship You." She began singing songs to the Lord. She didn't address the crowd. She didn't ask us how we were doing. The Lord was the center of her attention. For ninety minutes or so, she sang worship to the Lord like no one else was in the room, and we joined her. I can't remember the exact songs, but the refrains were similar to "Here I am to worship" or "I love you, Lord." The melodies reflected a collective of individual conversations with the Lord. Interestingly, she never prompted the crowd to sing along. She never encouraged the audience to take part. For well over an hour, the songstress, like Mary, ignored everyone else in the room and focused on singing unto her Lord. And the gathering corporately made Christ alone the center of our attention. I have never been a part of something so honoring to God.

Staring into the sun affects how we see. As we focus on this amazing light, we grow blind. Imagine, if we focused our lives not on activities, but solely on God. What if we began each day with Jesus as the center of our interest? Consider if we gathered with the Holy Spirit as the focal point of our every service. Not playing to the crowd, we'd lose sight of our fears, worries, and doubts. Focusing on Jesus, like staring into the sun, our faces would grow warm, and we would grow blind to everything but our Lord. Like Mary, we would have found the "greater thing."

This book aims to reorient us from living our lives for Jesus and awaken us to live in a way where, day-to-day, our purpose is interwoven with God's presence. It's a call for us to realize that God has *authored us with intent*, and that intent is meant to be lived with Him. Our Lord designed us creatively and uniquely. Not just so that we can be fruitful, or begin to reflect His image, or even glorify Him through change that only He could produce in our lives. Our Lord designed us to connect *with Him*, distinctly from anyone else who has ever lived on the planet. God created us not merely for salvation but for a personal and intimate relationship.

This is not a shared relationship. In comparison, our love for siblings, parents, spouses, even children doesn't register as a distant second. In the relationship between Christ and His bride, the church, there are new wedding vows and expectations. Not words meant to be mindlessly repeated, but intentions that are meant to bond our hearts inseparably to His. This wedding betrothal for each of us begins with a proposal to "come and see" (John 1:39). It's an invitation for us to walk away from our outer garments of money, independence, and Photoshopped lives and become exposed, vulnerable, and uncovered: getting naked before Him and learning to trust Him with our strengths and weaknesses. My prayer is that we'd grow beyond the charade of living *for* God. And we would embrace the abundant, purpose-filled life of living *with* God the Father; Jesus Christ, His Son; and the Holy Spirit in the fullness of His Divine nature.

Thank you for reading.

If you've enjoyed this book, please share it with a friend and write a favorable review on Amazon.com or BN.com.

Yours in Christ,

Berkley Baker

# The Four Blends of Divine Nature©

## EARTHLY COMMANDER

**DEFINITION:**
Earthly - pertaining to this present world

Commander - Ruler, authoritative

**CHARACTERISTICS:**
Conditionality (if...then)

Focused on earthly desires

Behavior logical and ordered

Relationship hierarchal and formal (i.e. King/Servant)

Communication consists of directives and commands

Choice is constrained

God is pleased through general/universal obedience

**THEME:**
Awareness - We become mindful of God

**OUTCOME:**
Productivity (healing, provision, deliverance, etc)

## HEAVENLY COMMANDER

**DEFINITIONS:**
Heavenly - pertaining to the world to come

Commander - ruler, authoritative

**CHARACTERISTICS:**
Conditionality (if...then)

Focused on heavenly desires

Behavior logical and ordered

Relationship hierarchal and formal (i.e. King/Servant)

Communication consists of directives and commands

Choice is constrained

God is pleased through general/universal obedience

**THEME:**
Adjustment - We strive to be like Christ

**OUTCOME:**
Conformity

## EARTHLY COMPANION

**DEFINITIONS:**
Earthly - pertaining to this present world

Companion - friend, participative

**CHARACTERISTICS:**
Unconditional

Focused on people, presently

Behavior incongruent, departs from human reasoning

Relationship collaborative, less formal (i.e. Bridegroom/Bride)

Communication consists of questions and dialogue

Freewill

Pleasing God is more personal and specific, may deviate from norms

**THEME:**
Abandon - We leave everything for Him

**OUTCOME:**
Transformation

## HEAVENLY COMPANION

**DEFINITIONS:**
Heavenly - pertaining to the world to come

Companion - friend, participative

**CHARACTERISTICS:**
Unconditional

Focused on people, eternally

Behavior incongruent, departs from human reasoning

Relationship collaborative, less formal (i.e. Bridegroom/Bride)

Communication consists of questions and dialogue

Freewill

Pleasing God is more personal and specific, may deviate from norms

**THEME:**
Authenticity - Changed by Him

**OUTCOME:**
Intimacy

# ENDNOTES

[i] "I Need Thee Every Hour," n.d.

[ii] "Abraham Wald." Wikipedia. Wikimedia Foundation, Nov. 14, 2019. https://en.wikipedia.org/wiki/Abraham_Wald.

[iii] Syed, Matthew. *Black Box Thinking*. (New York: Penguin Random House, 2015), 33-37.

[iv] Orthosie. "Quenya Translator." Fun Translations. orthosie. Accessed Jan. 18, 2020. https://funtranslations.com/quenya. Translation: "Like the donkey, I speak."

[v] Newport, Frank. "Church Leaders and Declining Religious Service Attendance." Gallup. Sept. 7, 2018. https://news.gallup.com/opinion/polling-matters/242015/church-leaders-declining-religious-service-attendance.aspx

vi Pew Research Center. "Why Americans Go (and Don't Go) to Religious Services." Aug. 1, 2018. https://www.pewforum.org/2018/08/01/why-americans-go-to-religious-services/?utm_source=link_newsv9&utm_campaign=item_242015&utm_medium=copy

[vii] "aware." *Merriam-Webster.com*. 2011. https://www.merriam-webster.com (4 Jan. 2020).

[viii] "adjust." *Merriam-Webster.com*. 2011. https://www.merriam-webster.com (4 Jan. 2020).

[ix] "conformity." *Google Dictionary*. 2009. https://www.lexico.com (4 Jan. 2020).

[x] "kowtowing." *Merriam-Webster.com*. 2011. https://www.merriam-webster.com (4 Jan. 2020).

[xi] "cognitive." *Merriam-Webster.com*. 2011. https://www.merriam-webster.com (4 Jan. 2020).

[xii] The New York Times, The New York Times, 3 Mar. 2000, archive.nytimes.com/www.nytimes.com/library/national/030400bobjones-edu.html?Partner=iVillage&RefId=LmyyW.

[xiii] Daniel G. Reid et al., Dictionary of Christianity in America (Downers Grove, IL: InterVarsity Press, 1990).

[xiv] "Oaths of Enlistment and Oaths of Office." Oaths of Enlistment and Oaths of Office - U.S. Army Center of Military History, history.army.mil/html/faq/oaths.html.

xv "incongruent." Incongruent Dictionary Definition | Incongruent Defined, www.yourdictionary.com/incongruent

xvi *Batman v Superman: Dawn of Justice.* Directed by Zack Snyder. (2013; Warner Bros. Pictures, Burbank, CA. Film.)

xvii Gladwell, Malcolm. "The Art of Failure." New Yorker, Aug. 21, 2000

xviii https://www.lexico.com/en/definition/unity

xix https://www.encyclopedia.com/science-and-technology/computers-and-electrical-engineering/computers-and-computing/heuristic

xx "abandon." *Merriam-Webster.com.* 2011. https://www.merriam-webster.com (4 Jan. 2020).

xxi "transformation." *Google Dictionary.* 2009. https://www.lexico.com (4 Jan. 2020).

xxii "What Goes on Inside a Cocoon?" Wonderopolis, wonderopolis.org/wonder/what-goes-on-inside-a-cocoon.

xxiii Lobo, Tricia. "How to Know If a Caterpillar in a Cocoon Is Dead." Sciencing, 18 Nov. 2019, www.hunker.com/12505822/how-to-know-if-a-caterpillar-in-a-cocoon-is-dead.

xxiv "Strong's Exhaustive Bible Concordance Online." Bible Study Tools, www.biblestudytools.com/concordances/strongs-exhaustive-concordance/.

xxv "authentic." *Apple Version 2.3.0.* 2018. (4 Jan. 2020).

xxvi "intimacy." *Apple Version 2.3.0.* 2018. (4 Jan. 2020).

xxvii Pasick, Adam. "China's 'Fast Food Homes' Were Built Quickly and Cheaply, and They're Starting to Collapse." *Quartz*, Quartz, 28 Aug. 2014, qz.com/196162/chinas-fast-food-homes-were-built-quickly-and-cheaply-and-theyre-starting-to-collapse/.

xxviii *The Break-Up.* Directed by Peyton Reed. (2006; Universal Pictures, Chicago, Ill. Film.)

Made in the USA
Coppell, TX
12 June 2020